American Book Company's

MASTERING THE

GEORGIA FIFTH GRADE CRCT

IN READING

DEVELOPED TO THE NEW GPS STANDARDS

Kim Hill

Dr. Frank J. Pintozzi, Project Coordinator

American Book Company
PO Box 2638
Woodstock, GA 30188-1383
Toll Free: 1 (888) 264-5877   Phone: (770) 928-2834
Fax: (770) 928-7483   Toll Free Fax: 1 (866) 827-3240
www.americanbookcompany.com

ACKNOWLEDGEMENTS

The author would like to gratefully acknowledge the formatting and technical contributions of Marsha Torrens.

Original graphics are the expertise of Mary Stoddard

This product/publication includes images from CorelDRAW 9 and 11 which are protected by the copyright laws of the United States, Canada, and elsewhere. Used under license.

ALL RIGHTS RESERVED

Table of Contents

vi

Grade 5 Georgia CRCT Reading
Preface

Mastering the Georgia Fifth Grade CRCT in Reading will help students who are learning or reviewing standards for the reading sections of the **Georgia Fifth Grade CRCT Reading** exams. The materials in this book are based on the GPS assessment standards as published by the Georgia Department of Education.

This book contains several sections:

    1) General information about the book itself

    2) A pretest

    3) An evaluation chart

    4) Six chapters that teach the concepts and skills needed for test readiness

    5) Two practice tests

Standards are posted at the beginning of each chapter, in the diagnostic and practice tests as well as in a chart included in the answer manual.

We welcome comments and suggestions about this book. Please contact the author at

American Book Company
PO Box 2638
Woodstock, GA 30188-1383

Call Toll Free: (888) 264-5877
Phone: (770) 928-2834
Toll Free Fax: 1 (866) 827-3240

Visit us online at
www.americanbookcompany.com

About the Author:

Kim Hill graduated magna cum laude from Kennesaw State University and taught English and Language Arts. She currently serves as a writer at American Book Company and works with at-risk students on the elementary reading level.

About the Project Coordinator:

Dr. Frank J. Pintozzi is an adjunct Professor of Education at Kennesaw (GA) State University. For over 28 years, he has taught English and reading at the high school and college levels as well as in teacher preparation courses in language arts and social studies. In addition to writing and editing state standard specific texts for high school graduation exams, he has edited and written numerous college textbooks.

Georgia 5th Grade CRCT Reading
Diagnostic Test

The purpose of this diagnostic test is to measure your knowledge in reading comprehension and critical thinking. This diagnostic test is based on the Georgia standards for English and Language Arts and adheres to the sample question format provided by the Georgia Department of Education.

General Directions:

1. Read all directions carefully.

2. Read each question or sample. Then choose the best answer.

3. Choose only one answer for each question. If you change an answer, be sure to erase your original answer completely.

4. After taking the test, you or your instructor should score it using the evaluation chart following the test. This will enable you to determine your strengths and weaknesses.

Each question on this test conforms to the Georgia ELA standard in the box next to it.

Read the following passage and answer the questions that follow.

excerpt from "The Chase" by Kim Hill

Michael and Adam ran swiftly through the overgrown brush that edged the forest behind their house. Ducking branches and leaping over ravines, the boys seemed to fly over the ground. Their sneakers and the cuffs of their jeans were already muddy, and the chase had only started five minutes ago. Adam held the leash firmly in one nimble hand, while Michael repeatedly yelled "Sam! SAM! Come here!"

It was the third time this week Sam had escaped the confines of the fenced-in yard. Michael, Adam's younger brother, had left the gate open the first two times. This time Sam had dug a small hole under the fence and squeezed through.

Once Sam got out, he was unstoppable. Like a racehorse released from the gate, Sam ran at breakneck speed. The boys could barely keep up. They could see him in the distance, running through a clearing in the center of the woods — a blur of golden red fur flashing in the sunlight.

"There he is Mike!" Adam yelled. "Try throwing those dog biscuits you have in your pocket at him to get him to come to us, and I'll put the leash on."

Michael threw a couple of the biscuits out, saying Sam's name a little softer now. "Come on, Sam. Here boy." Sam stopped and looked up, sniffing the air. The boys were only a few feet away now, closing in fast. "Throw him some more," Adam commanded. As Michael reached into his pocket for more doggie treats, a noise distracted him. Sam was looking intently at something behind the boys, with his ears up, his nose twitching wildly.

Looking behind them, Michael and Adam saw the massive bear at the same time. Dark and strong, the black bear stood at the edge of the clearing only fifteen or twenty feet away, its beady eyes settling on the boys. Pawing at the ground, the bear's claws dug into the hard earth, leaving deep red gouges. Never taking its eyes off the boys, the bear lifted its snout and began to sniff the air. Trying to catch the boys' scent to see if they were friend or foe.

Michael and Adam stood very still. Staring at the bear, they neither moved nor spoke, <u>paralyzed</u> by fear and unsure of what to do next. All their years of living in the woods, they had never encountered a bear. And he was so close. The bear watched the boys closely, looking almost curious. Opening its large mouth, the bear grunted several times, then let out a low growling, grumbling sound. Michael whispered through clenched teeth, barely moving his mouth, "What should we do?" Adam whispered back, "Stay still. Maybe it'll leave." The bear grew silent. The boys and the bear stared at one another in the sudden stillness of the forest.

A loud bark broke the silence. Sam let loose with one bark after another, "woof-!woof-! woof-!" running toward the bear, barking loudly. The bear backed up slowly, as Sam skirted around it, circling and barking. Lifting one massive paw, the bear struck out at Sam. But Sam moved quickly, dodging the blow. The bear continued to back up, Sam pushing him further and further away from the boys, until both he and the bear were out of sight, and all the boys could hear was Sam's frantic barking in the distance.

1. Why do Adam and Michael go into the forest?   5R1

   A. to go fishing
   B. to build a fort
   C. to collect firewood
   D. to get their dog

2. This passage can BEST be described as   5R1

   A. an essay.
   B. nonfiction.
   C. a short story.
   D. a folk tale.

3. Which of the following media sources would be the **BEST** place to look to learn more about bears?   5LSV2-C

   A. a newspaper
   B. a beauty magazine
   C. an encyclopedia
   D. a mathematics journal

4. Who is Sam?   5R1, 5R1-I

   A. Michael and Adam's dog
   B. a bear
   C. Michael's younger brother
   D. Adam's older brother

5. The conflict in this passage can **BEST** be described as   5R1-A

   A. man verses society.

   B. man verses machine.

   C. man verses himself.

   D. man verses nature.

6. What do Sam, Adam, and Michael encounter in the forest?   5R1

   A. a deer

   B. a bear

   C. a lion

   D. none of the above

7. After Sam and the bear disappear, the boys will most likely   5R1-G

   A. run home and tell their parents about what happened and to find Sam.

   B. play a game of hide-and-go-seek.

   C. stay in the forest and wait for someone to find them.

   D. follow the bear into the woods.

8. How did Sam get the bear away from Michael and Adam?   5R1-F

   A. He jumped up and down.

   B. He threw dog biscuits at the bear.

   C. He barked loudly and circled the bear.

   D. He trapped the bear in a net.

> "Staring at the bear, they neither moved nor spoke, paralyzed by fear and unsure of what to do next."

9. In this passage, the word *paralyzed* means   5R3-B

   A. frozen.

   B. excited.

   C. shriveled.

   D. agitated.

10. How many times did Sam escape from the back yard?   5R1-F

    A. 5

    B. 2

    C. 4

    D. 3

11. Which of the following is an example of simile?   5R1-E

    A. Looking behind them, Michael and Adam saw the bear at the same time.

    B. As Michael reached into his pocket for more doggie treats, a noise distracted him.

    C. Dark and strong, the black bear stood at the edge of the clearing only fifteen or twenty feet away, his beady eyes settling on the boys.

    D. Like a racehorse released from the gate, Sam ran at breakneck speed.

12. What happens first? 5R1-A

   A. Michael and Adam encounter the bear.

   B. Sam barks loudly at the bear.

   C. Adam throws dog biscuits at Sam.

   D. Michael and Adam try to catch Sam.

> **You do not need to refer to the passage to answer question 13.**

13. The graphic above would most likely be found in a(n) 5LSV2

   A. magazine about school life.

   B. advertisement for pencils.

   C. scary novel.

   D. a book about following rules.

Commando Robot

Characters: *Mom; Noel, an eleven-year-old boy; Chase, Noel's nine-year-old brother*

Scene: [Mom, Noel, and Chase are sitting on the couch watching a family program on television one evening. A commercial comes on about a new toy, the Commando Robot. The commercial shows a boy playing with the robot and making it blow up his little sister's dolls.]

Chase: Hey, Mom here's that commercial for the Commando Robot I told you about. Just look at what it can do and the cool kid playing with it. Man, I want one of those. All the kids at school want one too.

Noel: Yeah, it's really neat. Tom got one last week for his birthday *(looking at Chase)*. If we had one, we could make them battle. All the kids at school would want to play with it.

Chase: *(Chase imagines his friends coming over to play with the toy.)* Mom, can we get one of those the next time we go to the store? I have twenty dollars, and it only costs ninety. Can we?

Noel: *(chiming in with Chase)* Can we, Mom? I have fifteen, and we can share. That means you'll only have to pay like *(he puts up his fingers to do the math)* fifty-five dollars or something.

(Noel and Chase beg their mother to get it, Noel getting down on his knees.)

Chase: We'll be extra good and help with more chores.

Noel: And I'll wash the car!

Mom: *(smiling at Chase and Noel, and throwing up her hands to get them to stop begging)* Well, I'm glad you're both willing to work for something you want, but I'm <u>afraid </u>I'm not going to get it for you.

Noel and Chase: *(looking at each other, then their mother)* Why not?

Mom: It doesn't look like the kind of toy I want you to be playing with. It's violent. And why do you really want it?

Noel: 'Cause it looks neat in the commercials.

Chase: Yeah, and all the kids at school want one.

Mom: (*relaxed and reasonable*) Well, I don't think those are very good reasons. Sometimes television can be good, like what we're watching now or educational programs. But other times, it sends the wrong message. You think if you get that toy you'll be more popular with your friends, right? (*Chase and Noel nod their heads.*) The advertisers set it up that way. Look at the boy in the commercial, he's cool, like you said Chase. But you don't need the robot or toys to make more friends. Commercials can try to trick you sometimes, and you really have to look closely to see how.

Chase: (*looking suspicious*) Trick us? How?

Mom: Well, like cereal ads. They say a super sweet cereal is part of a balanced breakfast, when really it's not. It's really just a lot of sugar.

Noel: You're right. I've seen lots of those. I guess we have to be careful when we watch television.

Mom: Just look closely at what you see and ask questions about it. (*smiling*) I won't get you the robot, but we can go to the store and get a different toy tomorrow.

Chase: Great, mom. 'Cause I saw this commercial for a new Whacky Ball…

Noel and Mom: Chase!   (*all laugh*)

14. The author gives action and provides emotions for the characters by using   5R1-F

   A.   bold type.

   B.   all capital letters.

   C.   quotations.

   D.   parenthesis.

15. The purpose of the commercial is to   5LSV2-C 5LSV2

   A.   persuade viewers to buy the Commando Robot.

   B.   inform viewers of the risk of dangerous toys.

   C.   convince viewers the Commando Robot is educational.

   D.   entertain viewers with funny stories about toys.

16. Why did Chase and Noel want the Commando Robot?   5LSV2-B

   A.   because they think it will help them with their chores

   B.   because they saw a commercial about it on television, and their friends want it

   C.   because they want to use it in the science fair

   D.   because they want to learn about technology

17. What is Chase and Noel's initial opinion of the Commando Robot after seeing the commercial?   5LSV2-B

    A. They think it's a waste of time.

    B. They think it's silly and don't care if they get it.

    C. They think it's neat and they want it.

    D. They think it's funny and educational.

18. What is the setting of the passage?   5R1-I

    A. in the car

    B. in the backyard

    C. in the living room

    D. in the basement

19. In this passage, the word *afraid* means   5R3-H

    A. fearful.

    B. anxious.

    C. scared.

    D. sorry.

20. What is the main idea or theme of this passage?   5R1-G

    A. All commercials on television are negative.

    B. Commercials can be misleading and viewers must ask questions about what they see.

    C. The Commando Robot is a neat toy.

    D. Television can be educational.

Dangerous Predators?

Think sharks are dangerous? Although they are the ocean's most feared and fascinating predators, most sharks, such as the whale shark and the megamouth, are <u>gentle giants</u>. These sharks prefer to dine on algae and small fish rather than large prey and pose no threat to people.

<u>There</u> are, however, a few sharks that prefer larger prey and can be very dangerous to people. The most dangerous sharks include the great white, the hammerhead, the tiger shark, and the bull shark. These sharks have been known to attack humans. However, according to some scientists, shark attacks occur only about 100 times a year and out of those only 10 are mortalities.

In contrast, people kill thousands more sharks each year for food and sport than sharks kill people. Shark fin soup and steaks are popular delicacies in many countries. In America, the mako is one of the most popular items on the menu. Up until the 1950s, shark liver was used to create vitamin A supplements. Today, sharks are hunted for <u>their</u> fins and <u>their</u> cartilage. Certain shark populations have <u>decreased</u> so dramatically over the last decade <u>their</u> names have been added to the endangered species list.

From a shark's point of view, people pose a serious threat to <u>their</u> survival. So who's the dangerous predator?

21. What is the implied main idea of this passage? 5RI-F

   A. Sharks are dangerous hunters.

   B. Shark populations have decreased over the last decade.

   C. Sharks are not as dangerous to people as people are to sharks.

   D. Sharks have never attacked people.

22. What is the author's **MAIN** reason for writing "Dangerous Predators?" 5RI-G

   A. to persuade readers that sharks are a dangerous threat to people

   B. to entertain readers with interesting stories about sharks

   C. to inform readers that sharks are not as dangerous as people think

   D. to convince readers to swim with sharks

23. How many shark attacks occur   5R1-F
    each year?

    A. around 100

    B. 10

    C. 50

    D. too many to count

24. What is the concluding sentence   5R1-B
    of the second paragraph?

    A. There are, however, a few sharks
        that prefer larger prey and can be
        very dangerous to people.

    B. So who's the dangerous preda-
        tor?

    C. Up until the 1950s, shark liver was
        used to create vitamin A supple-
        ments.

    D. However, according to scientists,
        shark attacks occur only about 100
        times a year and out of those only 10
        are mortalities.

25. A word that has a similar meaning   5R3-I
    to *decreased* is

    A. lessen.

    B. rise.

    C. grow.

    D. improve.

26. A word that sounds like *their* but   5R3-I
    has a different meaning is

    A. there.

    B. they've.

    C. that's.

    D. through.

27. What is the BEST way to describe   5R1-D
    how this passage is organized?

    A. chronological order

    B. logical order

    C. compare and contrast

    D. there is no order

28. According to the passage, what   5R1-F
    was shark liver used to make?

    A. soup

    B. vitamin A supplements

    C. cartilage

    D. steaks

29. Who or what are the "gentle giants"   5R1
    described in the passage?

    A. the whale shark and Megamouth
        shark

    B. the great white shark and the bull
        shark

    C. fishing boats

    D. tiger sharks

The Thunderstorm
by Kim Hill

The storm came in suddenly
that warm April night
As I was just resting my head
and had turned out the light.
With my cat at my feet
And the covers to my cheek

When the lightning started crashing
And the thunder started clanging.
I sat up in my bed
and put my hands to my head.

It rattled the windows
and shook all the doors
The wind hissing and <u>moaning</u>
Through cracks under the floors.
It scared my cat
with its thunderous roars.

I sat and I watched
And finally drifted to sleep.
The storm <u>smoldered</u> and died
till not making a peep.

And echoes of thunder
Seemed to whisper goodbye.

30. This passage is an example of   5R1

    A. a folktale.

    B. essay.

    C. poetry.

    D. non-fiction.

31. Which of the following is an   5R1-E
example of personification?

    A. "I was just resting my head and had turned out the light. "

    B. "When the lightning started crashing"

    C. "And the thunder started clanging."

    D. "The wind hissing and moaning as it seeped through the cracks and the crannies in the floors"

32. In what time of the year is this   5R1-I, 5R1-A
poem set?

    A. spring

    B. fall

    C. summer

    D. winter

33. What is the rhyme scheme of the   5R1-H
last stanza?

    A. abbb

    B. abcb

    C. abab

    D. bbaa

34. Which word is an antonym for   5R3-I
moaning?

    A. sad

    B. unhappy

    C. joyful

    D. sorrowful

35. Based on the author's description   5R1-I
of the storm, we can infer that   5R1-F

    A. the storm was frightening.

    B. the storm was peaceful.

    C. the storm was enjoyable.

    D. the storm was playful.

36. In this passage, the word   5R3-B
smoldered most nearly means

    A. quieted down.

    B. strengthened.

    C. grew louder.

    D. built up.

37. Which of the following is the best   5R1-E
example of imagery?

    A. "The storm came in suddenly"

    B. "It rattled the windows"

    C. "I sat up in my bed"

    D. "And the thunder started clanging"

38. Which of the following best   5R1-G
describes how the speaker feels at the end of the poem?

    A. frightened

    B. calm and sleepy

    C. anxious and alert

    D. excited

You do not need to refer to the
passage to answer question 39.

---

39. Which word contains a prefix that
    means *away from*?

    5R3-C
    5R3-E

    A. unfortunate

    B. adjacent

    C. absent

    D. appropriate

The following passage comes from the novel *Anne of Green Gables* by Lucy Maud
Montgomery. In this excerpt, Matthew Cuthbert is on his way to the train station to pick
up a boy he and his sister, Marilla, have decided to adopt. However, there is a girl, Anne,
waiting for Matthew instead. Read the story about how Matthew and Anne meet. Then
answer the questions that follow.

---

excerpt from *Anne of Green Gables*
by Lucy Maude Montgomery

Matthew Cuthbert and the sorrel mare jogged comfortably over the eight
miles to Bright River…

When he reached Bright River there was no sign of any train…The long platform was almost deserted; the only living creature in sight being a girl who was
sitting on a pile of shingles at the extreme end. Matthew, barely noting that it *was*
a girl, sidled past her as quickly as possible without looking at her. Had he looked
he could hardly have failed to notice the tense rigidity and expectation of her attitude and expression. She was sitting there waiting for something or somebody
and, since sitting and waiting was the only thing to do just then, she sat and
waited with all her might and <u>main</u>.

Matthew encountered the stationmaster…and asked him if the five-thirty
train would soon be along.

"The five-thirty train has been in and gone half an hour ago," answered that brisk official. "But there was a passenger dropped off for you — a little girl...I asked her to go into the ladies' waiting room, but she informed me...she preferred to stay outside. 'There was more scope for imagination,' she said. She's a case, I should say."

"I'm not expecting a girl," said Matthew blankly. "It's a boy I've come for. He should be here..."

The stationmaster whistled.

"Guess there's some mistake," he said. "Mrs. Spencer came off the train with that girl...Said you and your sister were adopting her from an orphan asylum and that you would be along for her presently. That's all I know about it — and I haven't got any more orphans concealed hereabouts."

"I don't understand," said Matthew helplessly . . .

"Well, you'd better question the girl," said the stationmaster carelessly. "I dare say she'll be able to explain — she's got a tongue of her own, that's certain...Maybe they were out of boys of the brand you wanted."

Matthew groaned in spirit as he turned about and shuffled gently down the platform towards her.

She had been watching him ever since he had passed her and she had her eyes on him now. Matthew was not looking at her and would not have seen what she was really like if he had been, but an ordinary observer would have seen this: A child of about eleven, garbed in a very short, very tight, very ugly dress...She wore a faded brown sailor hat and extending down her back were two braids of very thick, decidedly red hair. Her face was small, white and thin, also much freckled; her mouth was large and so were her eyes, which looked green in some lights and gray in others.

An extraordinary observer might have seen that the chin was very pointed and pronounced; that the big eyes were full of spirit and vivacity; that the mouth was sweet-lipped and expressive; that the forehead was broad and full; in short, our discerning extraordinary observer might have concluded that no commonplace soul inhabited the body of this stray woman-child of whom shy Matthew Cuthbert was so ludicrously afraid.

Matthew…was spared the ordeal of speaking first, for as soon as she concluded that he was coming to her she stood up, with one thin brown hand the handle of grasping a shabby, old-fashioned carpet-bag; the other she held out to him.

"I suppose you are Mr. Matthew Cuthbert of Green Gables?" she said in a peculiarly clear, sweet voice. "I'm very glad to see you. I was beginning to be afraid you weren't coming for me and I was imagining all the things that might have happened to prevent you. I had made up my mind that if you didn't come for me to-night I'd go down the track to that big wild cherry tree at the bend, and climb up into it to stay all night. I wouldn't be a bit afraid, and it would be lovely to sleep in a wild cherry tree all white with bloom in the moonshine, don't you think? You could imagine you were dwelling in marble halls, couldn't you? And I was quite sure you would come for me in the morning, if you didn't to-night."

Matthew had taken the scrawny little hand awkwardly in his; then and there he decided what to do. He could not tell this child with the glowing eyes that there had been a mistake; he would take her home and let Marilla do that. She couldn't be left at Bright River anyhow, no matter what <u>mistake</u> had been made, so all questions and explanations might as well be deferred until he was safely back at Green Gables.

"I'm sorry I was late," he said shyly.

40. The author lets the reader know that this passage is set in the past by   5RI-D

   A. describing the horse and the train station.

   B. including a discussion about local plant life.

   C. mentioning the cars on the road.

   D. describing the little girl's face.

41. According to the passage, what "mistake" had been made?   5RI

   A. The orphanage sent a girl instead of a boy.

   B. The five-thirty train was late.

   C. Matthew went to the wrong train station.

   D. The stationmaster didn't know anything about trains.

42. Which of the following BEST describes how this passage is organized?   5R1-D

    A. cause and effect

    B. compare and contrast

    C. chronological

    D. none of the above

43. This passage portrays the little girl, Anne, as   5R1-I

    A. withdrawn and quiet.

    B. fearful and nervous.

    C. talkative and imaginative.

    D. sad and shy.

44. Where was the little girl going to sleep if Matthew never came to get her from the train station?   5R1-I

    A. in a wild cherry tree

    B. by the train tracks

    C. on a pile of shingles

    D. on her bag

45. What does the stationmaster mean when he says, "She's got a tongue of her own, that's certain."   5R1-E

    A. The girl is able to speak for herself.

    B. The girl is willful.

    C. The girl likes to stick out her tongue.

    D. The girl likes to tell lies.

46. What is the setting of this passage?   5R1-A

    A. a busy city train station

    B. a train station in the countryside

    C. a bus station

    D. a truck stop

47. Which of the following is an example of dialogue?   5R1-F

    A. She was sitting there waiting for something or somebody and, since sitting and waiting was the only thing to do just then, she sat and waited with all her might and main.

    B. The long platform was almost deserted; the only living creature in sight being a girl who was sitting on a pile of shingles at the extreme end.

    C. "I suppose you are Mr. Matthew Cuthbert of Green Gables?" she said in a peculiarly clear, sweet voice.

    D. Matthew had taken the scrawny little hand awkwardly in his; then and there he decided what to do.

48. What is the first sentence of the fifth paragraph?   5R1-B

    A. "Well, you'd better question the girl," said the stationmaster carelessly.

    B. "I'm sorry I was late," he said shyly.

    C. Matthew groaned in spirit as he turned about and shuffled gently down the platform towards her.

    D. "I'm not expecting a girl," said Matthew blankly.

49. Which of the following BEST   5R1-G
describes how Matthew feels
about the girl at the end of the passage?

    A. furious and upset

    B. depressed and gloomy

    C. shy and timid

    D. energetic and lively

"She was sitting there waiting for
something or somebody and, since
sitting and waiting was the only thing to
do just then, she sat and waited with all
her might and main."

50. In this sentence, the word *main*   5R3-B
means

    A. puny.

    B. heart.

    C. slight.

    D. little.

GEORGIA 5TH GRADE CRCT READING EVALUATION CHART

Directions: On the following chart, circle the question numbers that you answered incorrectly and evaluate the results. Then turn to the appropriate topics (organized by chapters), read the explanations and complete the exercises. Review other chapters as necessary. Finally, complete the **two practice tests** to further prepare yourself for the Georgia 5th Grade CRCT Reading test.

Note: Some question numbers will appear under multiple chapters because those questions require demonstration of multiple skills.

Chapters	Questions
Chapter 1: Reading for Comprehension	4, 5, 7, 8, 14, 16, 18, 20, 21, 22, 32, 35, 38, 40, 41, 43, 46, 47, 49
Chapter 2: Reading for Information	1, 2, 4, 6, 7, 10, 12, 20, 22, 24, 27, 28, 40, 41, 42, 44, 48
Chapter 3: Prose and Poetry	1, 2, 4, 6, 11, 29, 30, 33
Chapter 4: Figurative Language	11, 29, 30, 31, 37, 45
Chapter 5: Vocabulary	9, 19, 25, 26, 34, 36, 39, 50
Chapter 6: Media	3, 13, 15, 16, 17

Chapter 1
Reading for Comprehension

This chapter covers Georgia standard(s)

ELA5R1-F	analyze main ideas; determine main ideas; interpret the author's use of description; interpret the author's use of dialogue
ELA5R1-G	understand that theme refers to the implied or stated main idea; determine the author's purpose or intent
ELA5R1-A	identify the elements of setting; identify the elements of characterization; identify the elements of the plot and the conflict
ELA5R1-I	make judgements and inferences about setting, characters, and events

The CRCT will test how well you understand (comprehend) what you read. You will read passages and answer questions about what you've read. Then you will choose the best answer — A, B, C or D. The test will ask you many different kinds of questions. In this chapter, we will practice answering some of the questions you will see on the test. Once you know what kind of questions you will be asked and how to answer them, you *should* pass the test with flying colors! You'll be a better reader too! So let's get started.

MAIN IDEA — THE BIG IDEA

> **In this section, we'll answer the following test question: "What is the main idea of this passage?"**

The **main idea** is what the passage is all about. It is the point of the passage. Sometimes you can find the main idea in the title, for example, the title "What I did for Summer Vacation." This passage will be about what happened over the summer. It is the "big idea" of the passage. Other times, the main idea can be a sentence at the beginning or end of a passage: For example, the sentence "Children should have

Reading for Comprehension

more recess so they can be healthier" could be at the beginning or end of a passage. This sentence lets you know that the main idea is how recess is good for a child's health. In these examples, the main idea is stated. Now that you know what main idea is, let's practice.

Practice 1: Main Idea

Read the passages and choose the main idea. The first one has been done for you.

My Backyard

My backyard has slimy worms, creepy centipedes, spiders and jet-black beetles. I've seen crickets and grasshoppers too. My backyard has lots of neat bugs.

1. **What is the main idea of this passage?**

    A.   Slimy worms like to live in backyards.

    B.   My backyard has lots of neat bugs.

    C.   Crickets and grasshoppers like to eat grass.

    D.   My Backyard.

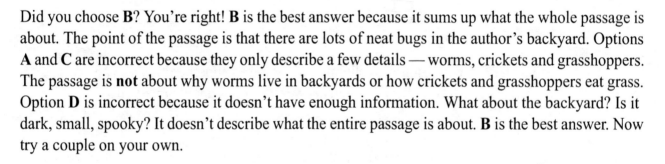

Did you choose **B**? You're right! **B** is the best answer because it sums up what the whole passage is about. The point of the passage is that there are lots of neat bugs in the author's backyard. Options **A** and **C** are incorrect because they only describe a few details — worms, crickets and grasshoppers. The passage is **not** about why worms live in backyards or how crickets and grasshoppers eat grass. Option **D** is incorrect because it doesn't have enough information. What about the backyard? Is it dark, small, spooky? It doesn't describe what the entire passage is about. **B** is the best answer. Now try a couple on your own.

A Great Snack

Apples are a delicious and healthy snack. They can be red, yellow or green and can taste sweet or tart or both. Packed with vitamins, they are a great food to eat every day.

2. **What is the main idea of this passage?**

    A.   Apples are red, green and yellow.

    B.   Apples are full of vitamins.

    C.   Apples are a delicious and healthy snack.

    D.   Apples are sweet and tart.

The Beach

There are lots of neat things to do at the beach. You can swim or make a sandcastle. You can also look for neat seashells or dig for clams. You can play volleyball too.

3. **What is the main idea of this passage?**

    A. You can swim or make sandcastles at the beach.

    B. You can look for seashells or clams at the beach.

    C. You can play volleyball at the beach.

    D. There are lots of things to do at the beach.

IMPLIED MAIN IDEA — READING BETWEEN THE LINES

> **In this section, we will answer the following test question: "What is the implied main idea of this passage?"**

Some passages you read will have a sentence that sums up the main idea, like the questions in practice 1. In many passages, however, the main idea is not written down in black and white. The main idea is not stated. It is implied. A passage with an **implied main idea** does not have a sentence that sums up the main idea. To figure out what the implied main idea is, look at the details to find out what the passage is about and the point it's making.

Practice 2: Implied Main Idea

Read the passages and choose the implied main idea. The first one has been done for you.

Good Volcanoes?

Volcanoes are not always destructive. Sick people take baths in hot springs warmed by volcanoes to feel better. Hardened lava or pumice can smooth the rough skin on your feet. Farmers use soil with volcanic rock and ash to help plants grow.

1. **What is the implied main idea in this passage?**

    A. Volcanoes can be helpful to people.

    B. Hardened lava helps your skin feel smooth.

    C. Volcanic rock and ash are harmful.

    D. Bathing in hot springs can be too hot.

Reading for Comprehension

Did you choose **A**? You're right! **A** is correct because it sums up what the passage is about. Options **B**, **C** and **D** are incorrect because they do not sum up what the entire passage is about. The point of the passage is that volcanoes can be helpful to people. **A** is the best answer. Now try a couple on your own.

What to Drink?

What do you usually reach for when you go to the fridge? Soda or water? If it's always soda, you could be making the wrong choice. Soda is full of sugar, has no nutrients and can make you hyper. Water increases your energy and keeps you hydrated. The next time you go to the fridge, pick water.

2. **What is the implied main idea in this passage?**

   A. Soda is bad for you.

   B. Water is better for you than soda.

   C. Soda is better for you than water.

   D. Water can give you energy.

Let's Play!

Soccer is a great sport to play. Soccer players have to learn how to kick and pass the ball. The goalie has to learn how to stop the ball. Most importantly, each player has to learn how to work together as a team.

3. **What is the implied main idea of this passage?**

   A. Soccer players learn many things when they play soccer.

   B. Soccer players have to learn to work together.

   C. You have to know how to kick and pass a ball to play soccer.

   D. You have to know how to stop a ball to play soccer.

THEME — EQUALS MAIN IDEA AND IMPLIED MAIN IDEA

> **In this section, we will answer the following test question: "What is the theme of this passage?"**

Main idea and implied main idea are sometimes called **theme**. On the CRCT, you will be asked, "What is the theme of this passage?" Do not panic. On the test, theme is the same thing as main idea and implied main idea. When you see the word "theme," think main or implied main idea and answer the question. For example, look at the passage below.

Last summer my family went camping. We set up our tent next to the river. We even caught a fish in the river the next day. At night, we roasted marshmallows and told scary stories. Our family camping trip was fun.

1. **What is the theme of this passage?**

    A. Fishing is fun.
    B. The best place to set up a tent is by a river.
    C. Camping with family can be fun.
    D. Roasting marshmallows and telling scary stories is the best part about camping.

The correct answer is **C**. Options **A**, **B** and **D** do not describe what the entire passage is about. They describe details about the camping trip. The passage is about how much fun the family camping trip was. The best answer is **C**.

AUTHOR'S PURPOSE — WHY WRITE?

> **In this section, we will answer the following test question: "What is the author's purpose or reason for writing this passage?"**

Author's **purpose** is the reason why an author writes. The author has something to say and a point (main idea) to make. When you read a passage, ask yourself, "Why did the author write this anyway? What is the reason?" There are many reasons why an author writes. They can write to inform or teach. They can write to entertain. They can also write to try to convince or persuade people to do or not do something.

Practice 3: Author's Purpose

Read the passages and choose the author's purpose. The first one has been done for you.

The curtain came up. The lights came on. I was prepared. I'd studied every word in the dictionary. "Barney Blosgow!" the announcer shouted. I reached the microphone at the center of the stage. I looked at the panel of judges, ready to spell my heart out. "Mr. Blosgow," said one judge, "spell otorhinolaryngology." My mind went blank.

1. **What is the author's purpose for writing this passage?**

   A.   The author's purpose is to inform.

   B.   The author's purpose is to persuade.

   C.   The author's purpose is to teach.

   D.   The author's purpose is to entertain.

Did you choose **D**? You're right! The author is trying to entertain readers. The author is not trying to teach, inform or persuade readers. The best answer is **D**. Now try on your own.

To start a flower garden you will need seeds, small starter pots, dirt, gloves and water. First, fill the pots with dirt. Then, bury the seeds in the dirt. Water them thoroughly every day. You should see little seedlings come up in a few days.

2. **What is the author's purpose?**

   A.   The author's purpose is to entertain.

   B.   The author's purpose is to persuade.

   C.   The author's purpose is to inform or explain.

   D.   The author's purpose is to amuse.

Vote for me on February 5th! I'll make sure we have soda for lunch and extra recess every Friday! I'll make school fun again! If you want more fun, don't forget to vote for me on February 5th!

3. What is the author's reason for writing this passage?

A. To persuade readers to vote for him/her.

B. To teach readers how to vote.

C. To inform readers when they need to vote.

D. To entertain readers with funny stories.

SETTING — WHERE AND WHEN A STORY HAPPENS

> **In this section, we will answer the following test question: "What is the setting of this passage?"**

The **setting** is where and when a story happens. Sometimes a story takes place in the future on a planet in outer space, like a science fiction book. Other times, a story takes place in England in the past. Understanding the setting can help you understand a character's actions and the main idea of a story.

Some authors use **historical** and **cultural** settings.

- **historical setting** — the story takes place in the past and may deal with a historical event.

  Example: A story about the soldiers in the Civil War.

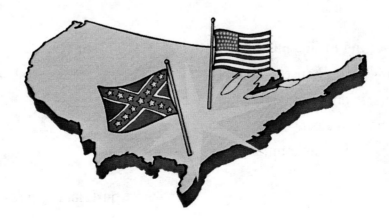

- **cultural setting** — the story takes place in the past and deals with a certain type of culture or way of life.

    Example: A story of a Native American living on a reservation.

Practice 4:   Setting

Read the passage and choose the setting. The first one has been done for you.

> The Martinez was sinking fast … Numbers of the passengers were leaping overboard. Others, in the water, were clamouring to be taken aboard again… A cry arose that we were sinking. I was seized by the consequent panic, and went over the side in a surge of bodies. How I went over I do not know, though I did know, and instantly, why those in the water were so desirous of getting back on the steamer. The water was cold — so cold that it was painful.

–From Jack London's "The Sea Wolf"

1. **What is the setting of this passage?**
    A.   The setting is in a house.
    B.   The setting is on a sinking boat in the ocean.
    C.   The setting is in a car.
    D.   The setting is in a swimming pool.

Did you choose **B**? You're right! The passage is taking place on a sinking boat. Now try a couple on your own.

The dogs were running at a good clip. Their black, gold and brown coats were the only colors against the white landscape. Snow had fallen heavily the night before and coated everything in a shroud of crystal white. "Mush!" my uncle cried. We were leaving the low valley, heading up the hills that circled Mount Episole.

2. **What is the setting of this passage?**

   A.   The setting is in a carriage in the woods.

   B.   The setting is in a snowmobile in the woods.

   C.   The setting is in a plane over snow covered ground.

   D.   The setting is in a dog sled on snow covered hills.

The air was dry and hot. "Are you sure we should go this far?" I asked Cindy. "Of course," she said. "If we want to see the deadly cactus in the valley, we have to." I was already parched and asked "How much further?" She pointed down the dusty hill, to a large cactus at the bottom. It was the only living thing in the sand-blown valley.

3. **What is the setting of this passage?**

   A.   at the beach

   B.   in the woods

   C.   in the desert

   D.   in the snow

CHARACTERIZATION AND DESCRIPTION: WHAT MAKES A CHARACTER?

> **In this section, we will answer the following test question: "How does the author describe the character in this passage?"**

Every person is different. We all have qualities that make us different from everyone else. The same is true for **characters** in a story. An author has to make characters different from one another so they are realistic to readers. Authors do this by describing characters. They describe how characters look, their age, how they act, how they speak and even how they feel. **Description** lets authors create characters and places in a story. Description can help you create a picture in your mind of a character or place in a story. You can also make judgments about characters based on how they are described.

Practice 5:   Characterization and Description

Read the passage below and choose the answer that describes the character. The first one has been done for you.

The man walked down the street, his feet shuffling slowly, his cane tapping against the pavement. Looking down, he silently counted his steps. At step ninety-nine, he stopped. He was in front of the house he grew up in. He looked at the big tree in front and remembered climbing it when he was a boy.

1.   **The author describes the character in this passage as**

   A.   a lost young boy.

   B.   a woman.

   C.   a crippled old man.

   D.   a healthy young man.

Did you choose **C**? You're right! The character in this passage is described as a crippled, old man. We know he must be crippled because of the cane he's holding. We also know he's old because he's walking slowly, and he's remembering when he was a little boy. The best answer is **C**. Now try a couple on your own.

Nancy was a beautiful girl. She glowed with excitement and wore a bright smile on her face. She was always moving or working on a project. If you looked away for a moment, you might miss something. She could send out 20 emails while your head was turned.

2. **How does the author describe Nancy in this passage?**

    A.   pretty and energetic

    B.   slow and stutters

    C.   ugly and hyper

    D.   pretty but lazy

Freddy Wallace walked down the hall, and everyone got out of his way. He was always looking for someone to pick on. Last week it was poor Sammy Samson. This week he was looking for someone new. When he tripped the new kid, Billy Bowden, we all knew he'd found another victim to bully for the week.

3. **The author describes Freddy Wallace as**

    A.   a friend.

    B.   a victim.

    C.   a bully.

    D.   a teacher.

DIALOGUE — WHAT CHARACTERS SAY AND HOW THEY SAY IT

> **In this section, we will answer the following test question: "Which of the following is an example of dialogue?"**

Dialogue is what characters say to one another in a conversation. You can usually identify dialogue by looking for quotation marks (""). Sometimes, a character may not be speaking out loud in a story. He or she may be thinking but not speaking. Many authors use *italics* when a character is thinking. Some characters may also speak with an accent. For example, if a character lives in the South, she may speak with a southern accent. What characters say and how they say it can tell you much about the story. It can help you figure out the setting and gives information about the character too.

Reading for Comprehension

Practice 6: Dialogue

Read the passage and answer the questions.

In this passage, Tom is pretending he's sick so he doesn't have to go to school. The plan backfires when his aunt realizes he's not sick, but that his tooth is loose and needs to be pulled.

"Well — your tooth *is* loose, but you're not going to die about that. Mary, get me a silk thread and a chunk of fire out of the kitchen."

Tom said: "Oh, please, Auntie, don't pull it out. It don't hurt any more… Please don't, Auntie. I don't want to stay home from school."

"Oh, you don't, don't you? So all this row was because you thought you'd get to stay home from school and go a-fishing?" …By this time the dental instruments were ready. The old lady made one end of the silk thread fast to Tom's tooth with a loop and tied the other to the bedpost. Then she seized the chunk of fire and suddenly thrust it almost into the boy's face. The tooth hung dangling by the bedpost, now.

But all trials bring their compensations. As Tom wended to school after breakfast, he was the envy of every boy he met because of the gap in his upper row of teeth …

– From Mark Twain's *The Adventures of Tom Sawyer*

1. **Which one is an example of dialogue?**
   A. By this time the dental instruments were ready.
   B. Then she seized the chunk of fire and suddenly thrust it almost into the boy's face.
   C. But all trials bring their compensations.
   D. "So all this row was because you thought you'd get to stay home from school and go a-fishing?"

2. **Based on the dialogue in the passage, do you think Tom and his Aunt have an accent? If so, what kind? Point out some examples.**

PLOT — THE MAIN EVENTS

> In this section, we will answer the following test questions:
> "What is the conflict in this passage?" *and* "What part of the
> plot is this passage describing?"

The chain of events that happen in a story is called the **plot**. The plot usually has several parts. There is an introduction, conflict, rising action, the climax, falling action and the resolution.

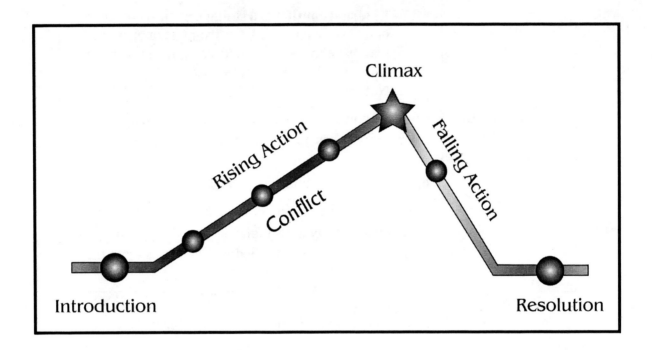

The chart on the following page will explain these parts for you.

Introduction	The beginning of the story. The author introduces the setting and characters.
Conflict	The problem or struggle the characters face in a story. There are two kinds of conflict in a story: Internal and external conflict. • **Internal conflict** is an emotional or personal struggle inside a character. For example, a character may have to overcome shyness. It is usually called **Man vs. Self.** • **External conflict** is a struggle against something outside of a character. For example, a character may have to survive a hurricane. It can be called **Man vs. Man**, **Man vs. Society** or **Man vs. Nature.**
Rising Action	The action in a story begins to build. For instance, a character who has been bullied may feel he doesn't have to put up with it anymore. He may start to prepare to face the conflict — the bully — in the story.
Climax	The climax is the turning point in a story. The action of the story is usually at its highest. For example, the character that has been bullied finally stands up to the bully.
Falling Action	The action in the story slows down. The character's life may begin to return to normal. It may even be better. For instance, the character that stands up to the bully is not bullied anymore.
Resolution	The resolution is the ending of a story. All conflict is settled.

Practice 7:   Plot

Identify which part of the plot each passage describes. Write introduction, conflict, rising action, climax, falling action and resolution for each passage.

1. Tom and Terry had been mountain biking for years. Every other Saturday they'd pack their gear and head out to remote mountain trails for a day trip . One weekend, they invited their friends Martin and Kasey to go with them. They decided they would ride a tough trail up the mountain.

    _____

2. Martin and Kasey had never been mountain biking. Halfway through the ride, Martin fell and twisted his ankle.

    _____

3. Tom and Terry knew they could make it over the mountain to get help, but they were unsure if they'd be able to find their way back. It was growing dark. They thought of what to do next.

    _____

4. Tom and Terry rode hard and fast over the mountain. The sun was sinking, and they were afraid they'd never find help. Exhausted and frightened, they were just about to give up hope when they saw a ranger.

    _____

5. The ranger, Tom and Terry made their way back to Martin and Kasey. Martin was carried down to safety on a stretcher.

    _____

6. As soon as they could, they called their families to let them know everyone was safe.

    _____

JUDGMENTS — WHAT DO YOU THINK?

> In this section, we will answer the following test questions: "What judgment can you make about the characters in this passage?" *and* "What inferences can you make about the characters or events in this passage?"

A **judgment** is your opinion about characters, events and the story itself. Did you like the story? What did you think of the characters? Were there mean characters or nice ones? Were there any events that made you happy or sad? The answers to these questions are your judgments about a story.

INFERENCES — MAKING A CONNECTION

When you make an **inference**, you are making a connection between what's said and not said in a story. Like implied main idea, an author may not state everything that happens in a story. He or she leaves it up to you to make the connection. For instance, look at the following passage.

> He held his breath and jumped in. The water covered his head and went up his nose. He could hear the muffled sound of his friends laughing and splashing around him. He opened his eyes under the water, looking around. He could see the yellow ring at the bottom through the clear water and swam swiftly toward it.

Did you guess that the boy had jumped into a pool? You guessed right. The author does not state this. You can infer the boy's in a pool because he's holding his breath, the water is covering his head and he's swimming toward a yellow diving ring.

Practice 8: Judgments and Inferences

Read the passage and answer the questions.

Most of the time Katherine was very loud. She was never mean to anyone, but she laughed and talked loudly when she shouldn't. While the teacher was teaching, Katherine would sometimes interrupt to ask a question without raising her hand. If someone said something funny, she would laugh so hard she couldn't stop. Once, she even had to write "I will not talk during class" on the chalkboard one hundred times.

1. **What inference can you make about Katherine?**

    A. She is shy.

    B. She is outgoing.

    C. She is easily frightened.

    D. She is a class clown.

2. **What judgment can you make about Katherine?**

    A. She's mean and likes to get other people in trouble.

    B. She is the teacher's pet and a good student.

    C. She never talks and never gets in trouble.

    D. She likes to talk too much, and it can get her into trouble.

I will not talk during class
I will not talk during class
I will not talk during class
I will not talk during class
I will not talk during class
I will not talk during class
I will not talk during class
I will not talk during class
I will not talk during class
I will not talk during class

I will not talk during class
I will not talk during class
I will not talk during class
I will not talk during class
I will not talk during class
I will not talk during class
I will not talk during class
I will not talk during class
I will not talk during class
I will not talk during class

CHAPTER 1 SUMMARY

DON'T FORGET!

Main Idea — what the passage is about.

Implied Main Idea — a main idea that is not directly stated in a passage. The details in the passage let you know what the main idea is.

Theme — Main idea and implied main idea are sometimes called theme.

Author's purpose — the reason why an author writes a passage. An author writes to entertain, to inform or teach or to convince or persuade people to do or not do something.

Setting — where and when a story happens.

- **Historical Setting** — the story usually takes place in the past and deals with a historical event.
- **Cultural Setting** — the story takes place in the past or present and deals with a certain culture or way of life.

Description — How an author describes characters, places, sights, sounds and even how things taste in a story.

Dialogue — words that characters speak to each other; conversation.

Plot — the main events that happen at the beginning, middle and end of a story. The plot has several parts. There is an introduction, conflict, rising action, the climax, falling action and the resolution.

Judgment — your opinion about characters, events and the story itself.

Inferences — making a connection between what's said and not said in a story. The author leaves out some information about the story. The details can help readers find what is missing.

CHAPTER 1 REVIEW

Read the following passages and answer the questions.

The Floating Princess

Once upon a time there lived a Queen and King in a far away land. They were very happy together, but had no children. The King grew frustrated when he noticed that other Kings in neighboring villages all had sons and daughters. The King asked his Queen angrily, "Why haven't you given me any children?" The Queen, being a kind woman, smiled and replied, "Be patient, my King."

The King did not wait long. The Queen soon gave birth to a baby girl. The King and Queen were very happy and wanted to share their joy.

They invited everyone in the kingdom to celebrate the joyous occasion. But the King forgot one person — his sister, the hateful Grethen. Grethen was one of those foul people who never had a kind word to say to anyone. She disliked everything and everyone. She had been cast out of the kingdom years ago. When she found out she had not been invited to the party, she was furious and planned her revenge.

On the day of the party, Grethen went to the party in disguise. She waited until she could see the little Princess. The King and Queen, unaware of the danger, walked up to every guest, showing their Princess. When they stopped in front of her, Grethen touched the child on the arm and began whispering strange words. The strange smell of magic filled the air. She finished speaking and blew a white feather at the little Princess. Then, in a swirl of dark smoke, Grethen disappeared.

Suddenly, the Princess began to float up to the ceiling. The King and Queen realized what had happened too late. The Princess had been cursed. She could not stay on the ground. She would fly about, as if on the moon. If someone bounced her on his knee, she would float to the ceiling and someone would have to bring her down with rope. For this reason she was never allowed outside.

1. **The main conflict in this passage is between the King's family and**

    A.   Grethen.

    B.   the Princess.

    C.   a maid.

    D.   the Queen.

2. **The author describes Grethen as**

   A. kind and gentle.   C. confused and scared.

   B. mean and cruel.   D. timid and shy.

3. **What is the author's reason for writing this passage?**

   A. to teach   C. to persuade

   B. to inform   D. to entertain

4. **Which of the following is an example of dialogue?**

   A. The Queen, being a kind woman, smiled and replied, "Be patient, my King."

   B. The King and Queen realized what had happened too late.

   C. The Queen soon gave birth to a baby girl.

   D. She finished speaking and blew a feather at the little Princess.

5. **Which of the following is the climax of the passage?**

   A. Grethen touched the child on the arm and began whispering strange words.

   B. They invited everyone in the kingdom to celebrate the joyous occasion.

   C. But the King forgot one person — his sister, the hateful Grethen.

   D. When she found out she had not been invited to the party, she was furious and planned her revenge.

Flightless Birds

Although penguins are birds, they can't fly. They waddle around clumsily when they're not in the water. Their wings are not designed for flight. They are designed for swimming. Their wings are powerful paddles that propel them through the water. Penguins swim at amazing speeds underwater.

6. **What is the implied main idea of this passage?**

   A. Penguins can't fly but they can swim very fast.

   B. Penguins are a type of fish.

   C. Penguins are clumsy on land.

   D. Penguins cannot fly.

7. **How does the author describe the penguins when they're on land?**

    A. graceful and swift

    B. sure and steady

    C. clumsy and wobbly

    D. robotic and precise

Taking Off!

The plane started down the runway. It went faster and faster. I looked out the window and saw the ground rushing past us. I quickly looked away. "We're going up soon," Dad said. I gripped the edge of the seat. "Relax. Flying is safe," he added. I could feel my head press against the back of the seat as the plane lifted off the ground. "We're up!" exclaimed Dad, excitedly. I closed my eyes.

8. **What is the setting of this passage?**

    A. in a space craft

    B. in an airplane

    C. in a boat

    D. in a helicopter

9. **What inference can we make about the main character?**

    A. He/she is scared of flying.

    B. He/she is excited about flying.

    C. He/she is quiet and shy.

    D. He/she is talkative and loud.

10. **What is the theme of this passage?**

    A.   Be patient and life will be good.

    B.   Overcoming fear is not easy.

    C.   Fathers always fly with children.

    D.   Flying in an airplane is safer than driving a car.

Chapter 2
Reading for Information

This chapter covers Georgia standard(s)

ELA5R1-B	understand and apply knowledge of textual features, such as paragraphs, topic sentences, and concluding sentences
ELA5R1-D	use knowledge of common organizational structures
ELA5R1-	read, recall, and analyze details and information from various texts
ELA5R1-G	make perceptive connections to draw conclusions; make perceptive connections to make predictions

The CRCT will ask you to read and recall details and information from different passages. In this chapter, we will learn how to break a passage down into parts to find information. We will learn what makes a paragraph, how passages are organized and how to draw conclusions and make predictions.

Learning how passages and paragraphs are organized will help you find information in a passage. You will also be able to draw conclusions and make predictions based on the information you find. In Chapter 1, we answered some of the questions you will see on the CRCT. Now let's answer some more.

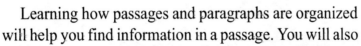

PARAGRAPHS — WHAT MAKES A PARAGRAPH?

> **In this section, we'll answer the following test questions: "What happens in paragraph one, two, three, four, etc...?"** *and* **"How many paragraphs are in this passage?"**

A **paragraph** is a group of sentences. Paragraphs are usually indented and start on a new line. A paragraph is about one idea. All the sentences in the paragraph should relate to that idea. Paragraphs have a beginning, middle and end. They have a **topic sentence**, **supporting details** and sometimes a **concluding sentence**.

TOPIC SENTENCE — WHAT'S THE PASSAGE ABOUT?

> **We will answer the test question: "What is the topic sentence of this passage?"**

As we learned in Chapter 1, the **main idea** is the point of a passage. The main idea can sometimes be found in a sentence in a passage. This is called the **topic sentence**. The topic sentence is usually at the beginning of a paragraph. It states the main idea of the passage. All of the other sentences are details that support the main idea. Below is an example of a passage with a topic sentence. See if you can spot it.

> I had a great summer. First, I slept in every day. I went swimming with friends. I stayed up late watching TV. I even went to camp! I wish summer would never end!

What is the topic sentence in this passage? "I had a great summer" is the topic sentence. It describes what the passage is about. Everything else in the passage supports the topic sentence. They are supporting details.

SUPPORTING DETAILS — THE NOT-SO-LITTLE THINGS

> **We will answer the test question: "Which of the following is or is NOT a supporting detail?**

Supporting details are what strengthen the main idea. Details are the facts, reasons and examples that support the main idea. An easy way to understand details is to picture a pyramid. The top of the pyramid is the main idea. The details are the base that holds the pyramid up. A pyramid cannot stand without a base. Likewise, the main idea would not be understood without details. Supporting details usually come after the topic sentence and make up the rest of the paragraph.

Let's look at the passage about summer vacation again. The supporting details are underlined.

> I had a great summer. <u>First, I slept in every day. I went swimming with friends. I stayed up late watching TV. I even went to camp!</u> I wish summer would never end!

The supporting details come after the topic sentence. They are the things (details) that let the reader know why the author's summer was so great.

CONCLUDING SENTENCES — WRAPPING IT UP

> **We will answer the test question: "What is the concluding sentence of this passage?"**

The **concluding sentence** is often the last sentence in a paragraph. It is the end of the paragraph. Look at the summer vacation example again. Can you find the concluding sentence? The concluding sentence is "I wish summer would never end!" It is the last sentence of the paragraph. If a passage has more than one paragraph, it is the last sentence of the entire passage. Now that you know the parts of a paragraph, let's practice.

Practice 1: Parts of a Paragraph

Read the paragraph below and answer the questions.

Volcanic eruptions can be dangerous and deadly. Eruptions can cause side blasts, lava flows, hot ash flows, mudslides, avalanches and floods. Eruptions have even knocked down entire forests. An erupting volcano can cause other disasters too, leading to *tsunamis* (large killer waves), earthquakes, mudflows and rockslides.

Because there may be hundreds or thousands of years between volcanic eruptions, people may not be aware of a volcano's dangers. When Mount St. Helens erupted in 1980, it had not erupted for 123 years. Most people thought Mount St. Helens was a beautiful, peaceful mountain and not a dangerous volcano.

1. **What is the topic sentence of this passage?**

    A. When Mount St. Helens erupted in 1980, it had not erupted for 123 years.

    B. Eruptions have even knocked down entire forests.

    C. Volcanic eruptions can be dangerous and deadly.

    D. Eruptions can cause side blasts, lava flows, hot ash flows, mudslides, avalanches and floods.

2. **Which of the following is one of the supporting details in this passage?**

    A. Volcanic eruptions are dangerous.

    B. Volcanoes are found in Hawaii.

    C. Volcanoes take 123 years to erupt.

    D. Volcanic eruptions can knock down entire forests.

3. **What is the concluding sentence in this passage?**

    A. Most people thought Mount St. Helens was a beautiful, peaceful mountain and not a dangerous volcano.

    B. Volcanic eruptions can be dangerous and deadly.

    C. Eruptions can cause side blasts, lava flows, hot ash flows, mudslides, avalanches and floods.

    D. An erupting volcano can cause other disasters too, leading to *tsunamis* (large killer waves), earthquakes, mudflows and rockslides.

4. **How many paragraphs are in this passage?**

    A. one

    B. three

    C. two

    D. none

ORGANIZATION — KEEPING IT NEAT

> **In this section, we will answer the following test question: "What is the BEST way to describe how this passage is organized?"**

When authors write, they organize their thoughts. They figure out the best way to get their point across to readers. Authors do this by using **organizational patterns**. Organizational patterns help authors arrange details and connect ideas in a passage. If a passage lacks organization, it makes no sense. For example, look at the passage below.

> As a result, we left the school late. Our backpacks, tents and sleeping bags were all over the school sidewalk. Finally, we arrived at camp. The buses arrived late. Our parents waved goodbye as we left on the bus. Ms. Conner announced a camping field trip.

This passage is confusing because it has no order. Authors avoid this by organizing their writing. There are many ways to organize passages. In this section, we will look at a few common ways authors organize passages.

CHRONOLOGICAL ORDER	When a passage presents events in order, from first to last or last to first, it is in chronological order. Passages in this order usually start with the first event, followed by the second, then a third and so on.

Example:

- **First event**: Fifth graders are invited to try out for the school talent show.
- **Second event**: Samantha decides she wants to sing in the talent show.
- **Third event**: She practices every day for the audition.
- **Fourth event**: At the audition, Samantha is nervous.
- **Fifth event**: Samantha gives a good performance and gets into the talent show.
- **Sixth event**: Samantha's parents take her out for pizza to celebrate.

Passages in chronological order often have KEY WORDS that let you know when events happen.

Chronological Order Key Words				
after afterwards as a Result	before finally first	last later next	once second then	third when

Now, let's go back to the passage about the camping field trip and put it in chronological order. Here is the correct order of events:

> Ms. Conner announced a camping field trip. Our backpacks, tents and sleeping bags were all over the school sidewalk. The buses arrived late. As a result, we left the school late.

> Our parents waved goodbye as we left on the bus. Finally, we arrived at camp.

CAUSE AND EFFECT	When one event causes another to happen, the events have a cause and effect relationship. A cause is why something happens. An effect is what happens. Sometimes key words such as *because, since, therefore* and *so* let you know the passage is in cause and effect order. When key words are not present, look at the events. Think about why the events happen.

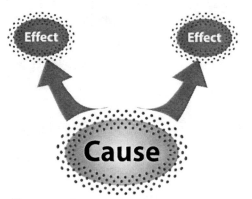

Practice 2:   Cause and Effect

Read the passage below. Then answer the questions. The first one has been done for you.

Forest Fire!

Imagine a dry, hot day in a forest. Dark clouds above build into a massive thunderstorm. The wind knocks branches to the ground. Lightning pierces the sky, striking a tall oak tree. The tree bursts into flame. The flames leap up to catch fire to other trees. The forest is soon engulfed in fire.

Is the forest destroyed? Not really. Forest fires can be another step in the forest's natural cycle. After a while, small plants and flowers will sprout again, feeding off the rich nutrients created by the fire.

1. **What caused the forest fire?**

   A.   a campfire

   B.   lightning striking a tree

   C.   a match

   D.   a flashlight

The correct answer is **B**. A bolt of lightning hitting a tree caused the fire. Now, answer the next one on your own.

2. **What effect did the fire have on the forest?**

   A.   The forest is burned but will re-grow.

   B.   The forest will never re-grow.

   C.   The trees in the forest are bigger.

   D.   The trees in the forest are greener.

COMPARE AND CONTRAST 	When authors compare and contrast, they emphasize the similarities or differences between the things or ideas in a passage. To compare, an author shows how things, characters or events are the same. They use key words such as *like*, *both*, *also*, *too*, *same* and *as*. To contrast, authors show how things, characters or events are different. They use key words such as *different*, *but*, *than*, *in contrast*, *however* and *unlike*.

Practice 3:   Compare and Contrast

Read the passage below. Then answer the questions. The first one has been done for you.

Movies or Rentals?

A movie theater has great sound. And the "big screen" is cool, but I think watching a movie at home is more comfortable. You can sit in your living room, talk and eat pizza. You can't do that in a theater. In contrast to uncomfortable theater chairs, you can stretch out on your sofa at home in your pajamas. You can even pause the movie if you have to use the restroom so you won't miss anything.

1.   **What is the author comparing and contrasting in this passage?**

   A.   apples to oranges

   B.   science fiction movies to comedy movies

   C.   books to movies

   D.   movies to rental videos

If you think **D** is right, you are correct! The author is comparing and contrasting movies to videos. Now try one on your own.

2.   **How is going to the theater different from renting a movie?**

   A.   Movie theaters and rental videos are both entertaining.

   B.   You can eat popcorn at the theater and at home.

   C.   Rentals don't have the big screen and great sound that a movie theater does.

   D.   You can go to the theater or rent a movie on the weekend.

LOGICAL ORDER

In a passage, each idea or thought builds upon the other. All of the sentences in the passage belong. They are all connected and revolve around the main idea. They follow a logical pattern. If they didn't, the reader may get lost or confused about what the author is trying to say.

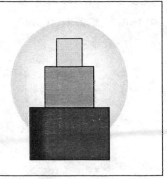

For example, look at the following passage:

> My mom locked her keys in the car. I like ice cream! It melted everywhere. It was chocolate too! We had to wait for the locksmith to come and open the car.

Does the sentence "I like ice cream!" seem out of place to you? It is. This passage does not follow a logical pattern. The passage begins by describing how the author's mother locked keys in the car and then talks about ice cream. The sentences about ice cream do not belong. They belong in another paragraph about ice cream.

CLASSIFICATION

In a classification passage, an author groups things into categories. An author groups ideas or topics together and discusses each one. It is usually organized like this: the first group, the second group, the third group and so on. For example, "Tourists in California can enjoy three kinds of water sports: swimming, scuba

diving and snorkeling." The author puts each water sport into a category and discusses each one. One category is not discussed more than the other. They get equal attention.

Look at the example below. Notice how the author puts his favorite animals into two categories: cats and dogs. The author talks about each one.

I like all kinds of animals. But my two favorite animals are cats and dogs.

I like dogs because they are loyal, and I can play fetch with them. You can take them to the beach too. And they like to ride in the car and stick their heads out the window.

I like cats because they snuggle up in my lap. When I drag a string around, they chase it. They're easy to take care of too. Just give them food and water, and they're happy.

READING FOR INFORMATION

Good readers are like detectives. They are able to pick out information in a passage to answer questions. When you read for information, look at the details to answer questions. To recall information and details from passages you read, you may have to look at a passage twice. If it's a long passage with many details, you'll probably need to read it again. Don't worry. Everything you need to answer the question is in the passage. Read the passage first. Then, if you need to, go back and look at the passage for the details and information you need. Let's practice.

Practice 4:   Reading for Information

Read the passage below and answer the questions.

The Dog-Eating Alligator

For 20 years, dogs have been disappearing in the Blackwater River Forest in Florida. The dog owners thought people were stealing their pets. They were wrong.

The thief, it turns out, was a 500-pound alligator. The alligator would grab dogs and eat them as they ran past him on a local trail. The huge gator ate at least six dogs.

One of the last victims was a dog named Flojo. Rufis Godwin, the dog's owner, had bought the dog for $5,000. The dog disappeared in the forest one day. The last thing Godwin heard from Flojo was her bark as she chased an animal.

After she disappeared, Godwin used the tracking device that came with Flojo's electronic collar to find her. The device would beep loudly as he got closer to his dog. Godwin got a faint signal. The beeps were weak. But when he reached a deep swamp hole, the beeps grew louder.

Jamie Sauls, who was with Godwin, also heard beeps coming from a collar worn by his missing dog.

"When we walked up to the swamp hole, we heard all this beeping," Godwin recalled. "So we knew we were dealing with an alligator." Gator hunters captured the 10-foot, 11-inch reptile on August 15.

1. **How did the dog owners find the alligator?**

   A.   They dug in the swamp.

   B.   They followed it through the swamp.

   C.   They used a tracking device.

   D.   They scared it out of a hole.

2. **How much money did Godwin pay to buy Flojo, his dog?**

   A. $500

   B. $2,000

   C. $11,000

   D. $5,000

3. **Who was with Godwin when he heard the loud beeping coming from the swamp hole?**

   A.   a ranger

   B.   Flojo

   C.   Jamie Sauls

   D.   an alligator

4. **What was Flojo doing before she disappeared?**

   A.   chasing an animal

   B.   swimming in the swamp

   C.   eating her dinner

   D.   sleeping on the porch

5. Where did the dogs disappear?

    A. Mississippi

    B. the Okeefenokee swamp in Georgia

    C. Canada

    D. the Blackwater River Forest in Florida

DRAWING CONCLUSIONS

> We will answer the question: "Based on the passage, we can conclude___"

When you draw a **conclusion**, you use the information in a passage to make a statement about a character or event. Like inference, a conclusion may not be directly stated. You make a connection between what's said and not said in a passage. You can draw conclusions based on how characters act and what they say, how characters interact and the setting of a passage. To draw conclusions, look at the details in the passage to form a statement about a character or an event in the passage. Let's practice.

Practice 5:   Drawing Conclusions

Read the passage below. Decide which conclusion can be made based on the passage. The first one has been done for you.

> John studied most of the week for the science test. He spent two hours every night going over definitions and exercises in his textbook. He slept well the night before the test.

1. What conclusion can we make about John based on the passage?

    A. John wants to do well on the test.

    B. John will fail the test.

    C. John will sleep late.

    D. John doesn't care how he does on the test.

Did you choose **A**? You're right. Based on the passage, we can conclude John wants to do well on the test because he studied hard and got enough sleep the night before the test. Let's practice a couple more.

We were deeper than we had ever gone. The pressure was unbearable. I imagined a tin can being crushed in someone's hand. Just when I thought the ship might crumple, the captain ordered, "Bring her up!" The crew threw back the switches, and the ship began to move up through the water. It took all the ship's power to get us to the surface again.

2. **Based on the passage, we can conclude**

   A.   the ship is going down into the ocean.

   B.   the ship is a fish.

   C.   the ship is rising up out of the ocean.

   D.   the ship is on land.

**Submarine in front of
Oceanographic Museum of
Monte Carlo, Monaco**

Do you think you lay perfectly still when you sleep? Think again. Studies show that everyone moves at least 8 to 12 times a night. People who have trouble sleeping move around even more. They can move 20 to 30 times a night.

3. **Based on the passage, we can conclude**

   A.   people never move when they sleep.

   B.   everyone moves at least 20 or 30 times a night.

   C.   people who have trouble sleeping shift positions more than people who don't.

   D.   people who have trouble sleeping shift positions less than people who don't.

MAKING PREDICTIONS

We will answer the question: "What will MOST likely happen next?"

A **prediction** is what you think will happen next in a passage. When you predict, you guess what will happen next in a story based on what has already happened. When you read a detective story, for example, you make a prediction when you say, "I think this guy did it!"

We make predictions every day. For example, we can predict the weather. If we see dark clouds gathering in the sky, we might predict it will rain. We can make predictions just like this when we read a passage. When you read, use what you already know and the clues in the passage to decide what happens next.

Practice 6: Making Predictions

Read the passage and answer the questions. The first one has been done for you.

Africa

 Many people think Africa is full of jungles, wild beasts, and people who perform strange ceremonies. Some think it's full of hunters dressed like Tarzan and throwing spears at zebras or elephants. But, Africa is very different from this. Africa is not just a jungle. It has deserts and grassy plains. There are not as many animals in Africa as some would think. Most of the animals live in protected areas. There are small villages in Africa, but there are large cities too. And many Africans dress just like we do in America.

1. **If you visited Africa, how would children most likely be dressed?**
   A. in sheets
   B. in robes
   C. in pants and shirts
   D. like Tarzan

If you chose **C**, you are right! The passage says, "Many Africans dress just like we do in America." Since Americans wear pants and shirts, many African children probably wear the same thing. Now, try the next one on your own. Then read "The Hunt" and answer the questions.

2. **If more cities grow in Africa, what will most likely happen to the animals?**
   A. They will disappear.
   B. They will only be in protected areas.
   C. They will move to the ocean.
   D. They will turn into people.

54

The Hunt

The five children started out, heading for the backyard. Carot directed everyone. They marched, counting their footsteps. Piper said, "The map says five steps west." The group turned left. "Then three to the north." They turned again. "That's it," Piper said. "We should be right on top of it." They looked down at the large X made out of black tape on the ground. Carot exclaimed, "We found it!" Pointing to Noel, he added, "Give everyone a shovel. Let's get started."

3. **What will the children most likely do next?**

   A. They will dig.

   B. They will continue marching.

   C. They will look at the map again.

   D. They will start fighting.

TYPES OF INFORMATION

Authors decide how they will present information to their readers. If they want to tell a story with characters and a plot, they write a **short story**. If they want to create a colorful picture in lines of sounds and words, they write a **poem**. If they want to explain a topic or give an opinion, they write an **essay**.

A short story or poem are considered **fiction**. They are ased on the imagination of the author rather than on facts. An essay is considered **nonfiction**. An author writes nonfiction based on facts and opinions. Newspaper and magazine articles are also examples of nonfiction.

CHAPTER 2 SUMMARY

Don't Forget!

Paragraph — a group of sentences about one idea. Paragraphs have a topic sentence, supporting details and sometimes a concluding sentence.

Topic Sentence — a sentence that states the main idea of the passage. Usually found in the beginning of a paragraph.

Supporting details — the facts, reasons and examples that support the main idea. Supporting details usually come after the topic sentence in the middle of a paragraph.

Concluding sentence — the last sentence in a paragraph or an entire passage.

Organizational patterns — the way an author organizes a passage.

- **Chronological Order** — when a passage lists events in order, from first to last or last to first.
- **Cause and Effect** — when one event causes another to happen. A cause is why something happens. An effect is what happens.
- **Compare and Contrast** — when an author emphasizes the similarities or differences between things, characters, or events in a passage.
- **Logical Order** — each idea is connected and revolves around the main idea. All of the ideas or details in the passage belong.
- **Classification** — when an author groups ideas or topics into categories and discusses each one.

Reading for Information — looking at details in a passage to answer questions.

Conclusions — putting information together to make a statement about a character or event in a passage. You can draw conclusions based on how characters act or what they say, how characters interact, and the setting of a passage.

Predictions — what you think will happen next in a passage. When you predict, you guess what will happen next in a story or article based on what has already happened.

Fiction — a work based on the imagination. Examples include the short story and poetry.

Nonfiction — a work based on facts and opinions. The essay or a newspaper or magazine article are examples.

CHAPTER 2 REVIEW

Read the passages below and answer the questions.

Tornado!

Tornadoes are the most violent and destructive storms on Earth. Tornadoes begin as strong thunderstorms and turn into funnel clouds. Winds from a tornado can reach over 300 miles per hour. They damage homes and down trees and power lines when they touch the ground. They can leave a path of destruction a mile wide and 50 miles long! Tornadoes can occur anywhere in the United States. But they happen most frequently in the Midwest and Southeast, an area called "tornado alley."

1. **What is the topic sentence of this passage?**

   A. Winds from a tornado can reach over 300 miles per hour.

   B. Tornadoes can occur anywhere in the United States.

   C. Tornadoes are the most violent and destructive storms on Earth.

   D. They can leave a path of destruction a mile wide and 50 miles long!

2. **Where do tornadoes most frequently occur?**

   A. in tornado alley   C. around lakes and oceans

   B. all over the United States   D. in the North

3. **Which of the following is NOT a supporting detail?**

   A. Tornadoes are powerful and dangerous storms.

   B. Winds can reach over 300 miles per hour.

   C. They damage homes and down trees and power lines.

   D. They begin as strong thunderstorms.

4. How large can the path of destruction left from a tornado be?

A. 20 miles wide and 1,000 miles long

B. 2 miles wide and 20 miles long

C. 1 mile wide and 50 miles long

D. 10 miles long and 5 miles wide

excerpt from Frank Baum's "The Sea Fairies"

(In this passage, Trot is going into a cavern in a boat. The cavern is beautiful, with a strange blue light coming from underneath the water. Someone calls her name. Trot is startled to discover it is a mermaid. Read about Trot's encounter with the mermaids and answer the questions that follow.)

Trot stared. Rising from the blue water was a fair face around which floated a mass of long, blonde hair. It was a sweet, girlish face with eyes of the same deep blue as the water and red lips whose dainty smile disposed two rows of pearly teeth.

Just at Trot's side appeared a new face even fairer than the other, with a wealth of brown hair wreathing the lovely features. And the eyes smiled kindly into those of the child. "Are you a — a mermaid?" asked Trot curiously. She was not a bit afraid. They seemed both gentle and friendly.

"Yes, dear," was the soft answer.

"We are all mermaids!" chimed a laughing chorus, and here and there, all about the boat, appeared pretty faces lying just upon the surface of the water.

"Are you part fishes?" asked Trot, greatly pleased by this wonderful sight.

"No, we are mermaid," replied the one with the brown hair. "The fishes are partly like us, because they live in the sea. And you are partly like us, but have stiff legs so you may walk on the land. But mermaids lived before fishes and before mankind, so both have borrowed something from us."

"Then you must be fairies if you've lived always," remarked Trot, nodding wisely.

"We are, dear. We are the water fairies," answered the one with the blonde hair, coming nearer and rising till her slender white throat showed plainly.

"Guess why we have appeared to you," said another mermaid, coming to the side of the boat.

"Why?" asked the child.

"We heard you say you would like to see a mermaid, so we decided to grant your wish."

"That was real nice of you," said Trot gratefully.

The brown-haired mermaid came to the side of the boat and asked, "Would you like to visit our kingdom and see all the wonders that exist below the sea?"

"I'd like to," replied Trot promptly, "but I couldn't. I'd get drowned."

"Oh no," said the mermaid. "We would make you like one of ourselves, and then you could live within the water as easily as we do."

"I don't know as I'd like that," said the child, "at least for always."

"Whenever you are ready to return home, we promise to bring you to this place again and restore to you the same form you are now wearing," returned the mermaid.

"All right, I'm ready, Miss Mermaid," said Trot. "What shall I do? Jump in, clothes and all?"

"Give me your hand, dear," answered the mermaid, lifting a lovely white arm from the water. Trot took the slender hand and found it warm and soft…

"My name is Clia," continued the mermaid, "and I am a princess in our deep sea kingdom."

Hans Christian Anderson's

"Little Mermaid"

in Copenhagen

5. **What will Trot most likely do next?**

A.   She will sail back to land.

B.   She will go under the water with the mermaids.

C.   She will yell for help.

D.   She will drown.

6. **Based on the passage, we can conclude Trot**

    A. is scared of the mermaids.

    B. does not like the ocean.

    C. does not like mermaids.

    D. is curious and excited about the mermaids.

7. **Why do the mermaids appear to Trot?**

    A. to convince her to leave the cave

    B. to tell her she is in danger

    C. to grant her wish

    D. to cast a spell

8. **What is the BEST way to describe how this passage is organized?**

    A. classification   C. compare and contrast

    B. cause and effect   D. chronological order

9. **What is the concluding sentence of this passage?**

    A. "All right, I'm ready, Miss Mermaid," said Trot.

    B. "Whenever you are ready to return home, we promise to bring you to this place again and restore to you the same form you are now wearing," returned the mermaid.

    C. Trot took the slender hand and found it warm and soft…

    D. "My name is Clia," continued the mermaid, "and I am a princess in our deep sea kingdom."

10. **What happens in the first paragraph?**

    A. The first mermaid appears.

    B. Trot asks if they are mermaids.

    C. The mermaids ask Trot to come to their underwater kingdom.

    D. Trot goes into the cavern.

11. **Who are the water fairies?**

    A. little fish under the water

    B. the tiny lights that flash in the cavern

    C. the mermaids

    D. the little girl

Chapter 3
Prose and Poetry

This chapter covers Georgia standard(s)

ELA5R1	explore literary works by identifying and analyzing elements of various texts
ELA5R1-H	evaluate the use of graphics, such as capital letters, stanzas, and lines in poetry; analyze the effects of sound to uncover meaning in poetry, such as rhyme scheme, onomatopoeia, and alliteration
ELA5R1-E	determine how poetry is affected by rhythm

We communicate with each other every day. We let our teachers and friends know what we're thinking through what we say or write. We call friends to ask them to come over to play, or send an email or card wishing someone a happy birthday. These are forms of communication.

Authors communicate through writing. Depending on what they want to say, an author may use everyday language (**prose**) or creative language (**poetry**). Authors have many tools that help them communicate ideas to readers: They use graphics, sound and figurative language. We use many of these every day. You may already be familiar with some of them, even if you don't know the correct term for them.

> **In this chapter, we will learn about some tools authors use in their writing. We will also learn the difference between prose and poetry.**

PROSE AND POETRY — WHAT ARE THEY?

Prose is what we write every day. When we send an email to a friend or write a book report, we use prose. Prose has paragraphs, sentences, and correct punctuation. Short stories, essays, newspaper articles, your schoolbooks and so on, are written in prose. For example, if you were doing a report on what eagles eat, it might look something like this.

> To hunt fish, an eagle swoops down over the water and snatches the fish out of the water with its talons. Sometimes, if the fish is too heavy, the eagle will be dragged into the water. It may swim to safety, but some eagles drown.

This example presents information in a straightforward manner. It is written in everyday language and has paragraphs and sentences.

Poetry does not have paragraphs and may not have complete sentences. Sometimes poetry does not have punctuation. Poetry expresses ideas, feelings or situations in a creative way. Look back at the example about eagles. If we had to write a poem about eagles, it would look very different. Look at the following example.

The Eagle
by Alfred, Lord Tennyson

He clasps the crag with crooked hands;
Close to the sun in lonely lands,
Ringed with the azure world, he stands.

The wrinkled sea beneath him crawls;
He watches from his mountain walls,
And like a thunderbolt he falls.

This **poem** tells us something very different about eagles than the prose example. It tells us something about the eagle's spirit or how it feels to fly or soar high above the world. Poetry says more than ordinary language (prose). Poetry is about words and associations. Poetry uses words that create mind pictures. For instance, the reader can imagine the majestic eagle standing on a mountain cliff. It can also make readers think, create feelings or emotions or look at something in a new way.

GRAPHICS IN POETRY — HOW POETRY LOOKS

A **poem** has stanzas, lines, capital letters and sometimes a refrain that prose does not. We will look at all of these below.

LINES

> **We will answer the test questions: "How many lines are in this poem?" and "What happens in line one, two, three, four, etc.?"**

Every poem has lines. Many times, there are numbers next to the poem that can help you count the lines in each poem.

Example:

1   Little Jack Horner

Sat in a corner,

Eating a Christmas pie.

He stuck in his thumb

5   And pulled out a plum,

And said, "What a good boy am I!"

How many lines are in this poem? There are six lines. If a question asks how many lines, just count the lines and answer the question.

STANZAS

> We will answer the test question: "How many stanzas are in this poem?"

A **stanza** is a group of lines in a poem. Stanzas are usually set apart by a space.

Example:

There was a little turtle
Who lived in a box.
He swam in the puddles
And climbed on the rocks. **1st stanza**

He snapped at the mosquito,
He snapped at the flea.
He snapped at the minnow,
And he snapped at me. **2nd stanza**

He caught the mosquito,
He caught the flea.
He caught the minnow,
But he didn't catch me! **3rd stanza**

There are three groups of lines in this poem. Each one is separated by a space. So, how many stanzas are in this poem? There are three. If a question asks how many stanzas there are in a poem, look for the space between a group of lines and count the stanzas.

CAPITAL LETTERS

> We will answer the test question: "Every new line in a poem begins with a _____?"

Every line in a poem starts with a **capital letter**. Look again at the two poems on pages 62 and 63. Notice how each line begins with a capital letter, even the word "And." Unlike everyday writing (prose), poetry does not have to have a complete sentence to have a capital letter. Each new line begins with a capital letter.

REFRAIN

> **We will answer the test question: "What is the refrain in this poem?"**

A **refrain** is a repeated word, phrase, or group of lines in a poem. It is fairly easy to spot a refrain. Just look for a repeated phrase or line in a poem. Poets use a refrain to add more meaning and emphasis to their poems. Look at the poem below for an example. The refrain has been underlined for you.

<u>I shall not live in vain;</u>
If I can ease one life the aching,
Or cool one pain,
Or help one fainting robin
Unto his nest again,
<u>I shall not live in vain.</u>

excerpt from *Life* by Emily Dickinson.

Practice 1:   How Poetry Looks

Read the following poems and answer the questions.

Falling Snow

See the pretty snowflakes
Falling from the sky;
On the wall and housetops
Soft and thick they lie.

5 On the window ledges,
On the branches bare;
Now how fast they gather,
Filling all the air.

Look into the garden,
10 Where the grass was green;
Covered by the snowflakes,
Not a blade is seen.

Now the bare black bushes
All look soft and white,
15 Every twig is laden,
What a pretty sight!

1. **How many stanzas are in this poem?**
   A. 5   B. 3   C. 4   D. 6

2. **What is described in the third stanza?**

   A.   The garden and the grass covered in snow.

   B.   The snow on the window ledge and bushes.

   C.   Pretty snowflakes falling from the sky and onto the rooftops

   D.   The bushes and twigs are covered in white.

3. **How many lines are in this poem?**
   A. 15   B. 16   C. 17   D. 20

Little Boy Blue by Eugene Field

The little toy dog is covered with dust,
  But sturdy and staunch he stands;
And the little toy soldier is red with rust,
  And his musket moulds in his hands.
Time was when the little toy dog was new,
  And the soldier was passing fair;
And that was the time when our Little Boy Blue
  Kissed them and put them there.

"Now, don't you go till I come," he said,
  "And don't you make any noise!"
So, toddling off to his trundle-bed,
  He dreamt of the pretty toys;
And, as he was dreaming, an angel song
  Awakened our Little Boy Blue —
Oh! the years are many, the years are long,
  But the little toy friends are true!

Ay, faithful to Little Boy Blue they stand,
  Each in the same old place —
Awaiting the touch of a little hand,
  The smile of a little face;
And they wonder, as waiting the long years through
  In the dust of that little chair,
What has become of our Little Boy Blue,
  Since he kissed them and put them there.

4. **Which of the following is an example of refrain?**

    A. "Oh! the years are many, the years are long,
        But the little toy friends are true!"

    B. "Each in the same old place —
        Awaiting the touch of a little hand,"

    C. "our Little Boy Blue
        Kissed them and put them there."

    D. "faithful to Little Boy Blue they stand"

5. **How many stanzas are in this poem?**

    A. 2   B. 3   C. 4   D. 5

6. **What is described in the first stanza?**

    A. The toys in Little Boy Blue's room.

    B. Dusty old toys on a shelf.

    C. Little Boy Blue tells the toys to stay still and be quiet till he comes.

    D. The toys wonder what happened to Little Boy Blue.

HOW POETRY SOUNDS — RHYTHM AND RHYME

When we talk, our words have a natural **rhythm**. We stress certain words when we speak without even knowing it. Look at the sentence "I want to play," for example. What words are stressed in this sentence? "Want" and "Play." They are the strong words in the sentence. The words "I" and "To" are not stressed. They are the weaker words in the sentence. If you could tap your feet to this sentence, it would be **tap TAP tap TAP**. The way we speak has a beat. The same is true of poetry. Poets use rhythm, **rhyme**, and **rhyme scheme** to give their poems a musical quality.

RHYME — WORDS THAT SOUND ALIKE

> **We will answer the test question: "What words rhyme in this line?"**

Words that **rhyme** sound alike. They do not have to be spelled the same, but they sound the same. Poetry often rhymes. We like words that rhyme. When we hear words that sound alike repeated over and over, we know we are reading a poem with a rhyme. It can be simple words like "**rat**" and "**cat**" or more complex like "**giraffe**" and "**carafe**." Rhyme makes a poem musical. Like the words of a favorite song, we can remember a poem more easily when it rhymes.

RHYME SCHEME — THE BEAT OF POETRY

If a poet decides to write a poem that rhymes, he or she creates a **rhyme scheme**. Poets have to decide what they want their poem to sound like. They create a pattern and arrange their words to fit into the pattern. The pattern of rhyming words in a poem creates a **beat**. This beat is the rhyme scheme.

Rhyme scheme is the pattern of rhyming lines in a poem. In a rhyme scheme, the words at the end of each line rhyme with one another. Letters usually stand for the rhyme scheme: **a** for the first two lines that rhyme, **b** for the second, **c** for the third and so on. Look at the poem below for an example. Look at the last word in each line to see the rhyme scheme. The rhyme scheme is marked for you on the right.

Twinkle, Twinkle Little Star (Rhyme Scheme)

Twinkle, twinkle little <u>star</u>, **a**
How I wonder what you <u>are</u>, **a**
Up above the world so <u>high</u>, **b**
Like a diamond in the <u>sky</u>. **b**
Twinkle, twinkle little <u>star</u>, **a**
How I wonder what you <u>are</u>. **a**

Notice how the last words in each line rhyme with one another. The words "star" and "are" are the first pair of rhyming words, so we mark them with an **a**. The second pair of rhyming words are "high" and "sky." We mark this with a **b**. The last pair of words rhyme with "star" and "are." We mark these lines **a** because they repeat the first rhyme of the poem.

Chapter 3

To find the rhyme scheme, pay attention to the last word in each line and how it rhymes with words in other lines. Try reading the poem aloud if you can. Sometimes reading out loud can help you figure out the rhyme scheme.

Practice 2: Rhyme Scheme

Read the poems below and answer the questions. The first two have been done for you.

> I went to town
> To buy a gown

1. What is the rhyme scheme of these lines?

    A. aa   B. bb   C. aaa   D. ab

Did you choose **A**? You're right. The words "town" and "gown" rhyme. Since there are only two lines, the rhyme scheme is aa. Let's try another.

Mary's Canary

> Mary had a pretty bird,
> Feathers bright and yellow,
> Slender legs — upon my word,
> He was a pretty fellow.

2. What is the rhyme scheme of this poem?

    A. aaaa   B. baab   C. abab   D. abba

Did you choose **C**? You're right again! The first pair of rhyming words are "bird" and "word." Mark them **a**. The second pair of rhyming words are "yellow" and "fellow." Mark them **b**. The rhyme scheme is **abab**. Try a couple on your own.

Hickory Dickory Dock

> Hickory dickory dock,
> The mouse ran up the clock,
> The clock struck one,
> and down he runs,
> Hickory dickory dock!

3. What is the rhyme scheme of this poem?

    A. aaaaa   B. aabba   C. babab   D. abbab

Where Snow Goes

The green things began to grow,
Poking through the slush that was once fluffy snow,
Where it went I do not know.

4. **What is the rhyme scheme of this poem?**

   A. aba   B. abb   C. aaa   D. aac

The Little Mouse

I have seen you, little mouse,
Running all about the house,
I can see your little eye,
In the wainscot peeping sly,
Hoping soon some crumbs to steal,
To make quite a hearty meal.

5. **What is the rhyme scheme of this poem?**

   A. aaaaaa   B. ababab   C. bababa   D. aabbcc

ALLITERATION — TONGUE TWISTERS AND MORE

> We will answer the test question: "Which of the following is an example of alliteration?"

Poets also use **alliteration** to create a certain sound in their poems. Many tongue twisters use alliteration.

Example: Peter Piper picked a peck of pickled peppers.

Notice how almost every word begins with a "P." This is called alliteration. When two or more words begin with the same letter in a line of poetry, it is **alliteration**. Identifying alliteration is easy. Just look for two or more words that begin with the same letter. For example,

Sally sold sea shells down by the sea shore.

Notice that first words in this line start with the same letter, **s**.

Not all poems with alliteration are tongue twisters. Remember you only need two or more words that begin with the same letter to have alliteration.

Example: The <u>s</u>un <u>s</u>ank below the <u>sh</u>immering <u>s</u>ea.

Example: <u>B</u>illy <u>B</u>ob was up to <u>b</u>at.

Example: <u>T</u>ina <u>T</u>weed had <u>t</u>omatoes and <u>t</u>ea.

Notice that the s, b, and f words have alliteration. Any repeated consonant in a line of poetry is alliteration. However, words that start with vowels are not alliteration.

Onomatopoeia — Bing! Bang! Boom!

> **We will answer the test question "Which of the following is an example of onomatopoeia?"**

When you cook popcorn, it *pops*. When wood burns, it *sizzles* and *snaps*. Words that imitate the sounds they describe are called **onomatopoeia**. Poets use onomatopoeia because it vividly expresses experience. Look at the examples below.

Example: The fly *buzzed* round my head.

Example: The air conditioner *hummed*.

Example: The fire *crackled.*

Practice 3: Alliteration and Onomatopoeia

Read the sentences below. Decide whether the sentence contains onomatopoeia or alliteration.

1. **The dishes crashed to the floor.**
   A. onomatopoeia   B. alliteration

2. **Frank flips perfect flapjacks.**
   A. onomatopoeia   B. alliteration

3. **Seven silly sheep slept on the street.**
   A. alliteration   B. onomatopoeia

4. **The engine whirred.**

   A.   alliteration

   B.   onomatopoeia

5. **The birds chirped.**

   A.   alliteration

   B.   onomatopoeia

6. **Sally said she would sew the sheets.**

   A.   alliteration

   B.   onomatopoeia

CHAPTER 3 SUMMARY

Prose — what we write every day. Prose has paragraphs, sentences and correct punctuation. Prose is used in articles, magazines, biographies, book reports, letters, books and newspapers.

Poetry — a creative way to express ideas, feelings, or situations. Poetry does not have paragraphs and may not have complete sentences. Sometimes poetry does not have punctuation.

- **Lines** — every poem has lines. Many times, there are numbers next to the poem that help you count the lines in each poem.

- **Stanza** — a group of lines in a poem that are usually set apart by a space.

- **Capital Letters** — every new line in a poem starts with a capital letter.

- **Refrain** — A repeated word, phrase, or group of lines usually found in poetry.

- **Rhyme** — words that have the same sound. Rhyme is most often used in poetry.

- **Rhyme scheme** — the pattern of rhyming lines in a poem. The words at the end of each line rhyme with one another. Letters usually stand for the rhyme scheme: **a** for the first two lines that rhyme, **b** for the second, **c** for the third and so on.

Alliteration — two or more words that begin with the same consonant in a line of poetry or prose.

Onomatopoeia — words that imitate the sounds they describe.

CHAPTER 3 REVIEW

Read the poems below and answer the questions.

The Vulture by Hilaire Belloc

The Vulture eats between his meals,

And that's the reason why

He very, very, rarely feels

As well as you and I.

His eye is dull, his head is bald,

His neck is growing thinner.

Oh! what a lesson for us all

To only eat at dinner!

1. **What is the rhyme scheme of this poem?**
    A.   ababcdcd
    B.   aabaacaa
    C.   abcabcab
    D.   baabaaba

2. **How many lines are in this poem?**
    A. 7   B. 6   C. 8   D. 10

Our Little Ghost by Louisa May Alcott

Oft, in the silence of the night,
    When the lonely moon rides high,
When wintry winds are whistling,
    And we hear the owl's shrill cry,
5   In the quiet, dusky chamber,
    By the flickering firelight,
Rising up between two sleepers,
    Comes a spirit all in white.

A winsome little ghost it is,
10   Rosy-cheeked, and bright of eye; 10
With yellow curls all breaking loose
    From the small cap pushed awry.
Up it climbs among the pillows,
    For the "big dark" brings no dread,
15 And a baby's boundless fancy
    Makes a kingdom of a bed.

A fearless little ghost it is;
    Safe the night seems as the day;
The moon is but a gentle face,
20   And the sighing winds are gay.
The solitude is full of friends,
    And the hour brings no regrets;
For, in this happy little soul,
    Shines a sun that never sets.

3. How many stanzas are in this poem?
A. 2   B. 4   C. 1   D. 3

4. How many lines are in this poem?
A. 24   B. 34   C. 40   D. 20

5. **Every line in this poem begins with a**

    A. space.

    B. paragraph.

    C. capital letter.

    D. stanza.

    > "When wintry winds are whistling"

6. **The line above is an example of**

    A. prose.

    B. alliteration.

    C. rhythm.

    D. rhyme scheme.

You do not need to refer to the poem on page 75 to answer questions 7 through 9.

7. **Which of the following is an example of onomatopoeia?**

    A. The rain fell.

    B. The sun rose.

    C. The frog croaked.

    D. The birds flew.

8. **Alliteration is**

    A. two or more words that begin with the same consonant and sound.

    B. a repeated phrase or line in a poem.

    C. a word that imitates the sound it describes.

    D. the way we write every day.

9. **What is rhyme?**

    A. the pattern of rhyming lines in a poem that creates a beat

    B. a creative way to express ideas, thoughts or feelings

    C. words that have the same sound in poem, such as bat and mat

    D. a group of lines in a poem set apart by a space

excerpt from Edgar Allen Poe's "Annabel Lee"

"For the moon never beams without bringing me dreams
Of the beautiful Annabel Lee;
And the stars never rise but I see the bright eyes
Of the beautiful Annabel Lee"

10. **Which of the following is an example of refrain?**

    A. "For the moon never beams without bringing me dreams"

    B. "And the stars never rise but I see the bright eyes"

    C. "Of the beautiful Annabel Lee"

    D. None of the above

11. **The words "beams" and "dreams" in this poem are**

    A. rhyme.

    B. alliteration.

    C. onomatopoeia.

    D. stanzas.

Chapter 4
Figurative Language

This chapter covers Georgia standard(s)

EIA5R1-E (GA GPS Web site)	identifies imagery, figurative language (e.g., personification, metaphor, simile, hyperbole), rhythm, or flow when responding to literature
ELA5R1-E	determine how meaning in prose and poetry is affected by imagery, figurative language, personification, simile, metaphor, and hyperbole

As we discussed in the previous chapter, writers of prose and poetry try to communicate an experience or emotion to readers. They want to create a feeling, an image or to make ordinary experiences seem exciting and new. Authors often use figurative language to help them do this. **Figurative language** uses words in ways that mean more than the dictionary definition. In other words, figurative language doesn't mean *exactly* what it says. For example, when we say "time flies," we don't really mean that time has somehow sprouted wings and is flying around. What we mean is time is going by quickly. Here are a few more examples of figurative language: *Walking on eggshells. It's in the bag. Spill the beans.*

We use figurative language every day. Many times we don't even realize we're using it. When we want to add emphasis to something, we may exaggerate (**hyperbole**): For instance, "Tim threw the ball so fast and hard it landed in Alabama." Or we may compare things to deepen our meaning (**simile**): "My mom is like an angel watching over me." Since figurative language comes so naturally to us, learning more about it should be a piece of cake!

Although there are many different kinds of figurative language, you only have to know a few for the CRCT. In this chapter, we will learn about **imagery**, **personification, hyperbole**, **simile** and **metaphor**. Let's get ready to learn how to answer more CRCT questions!

IMAGERY — DESCRIBING THE SENSES

> We will answer the test question: "Which of the following is an example of imagery?"

Imagery consists of words that express sight, touch, sound, smell or taste. Imagery describes what we experience with our five senses. An author writing a poem about spring, for example, would describe what we touch, smell, taste, hear and see during the spring. The author might describe the clear blue of the sky (eyes), the smell of fresh flowers (nose), the feel of a warm breeze (skin), the taste of lemonade (tongue) or the sound of children playing (ears). Like a painter, an author creates a picture in our mind through our senses. We may like certain poems because we can "see" or "feel" what they mean. Oftentimes, imagery paints a new picture of something ordinary. For example, look at the poem below.

Web in the Windowsill

There's a web on my windowsill,

I watch it as the soft rain falls

The web breathes in and out with the wind.

The spider clings in the center,

Like the dot in the middle of a flower.

The rain speckles the web with crystal jewels —

That drape and drip from each fine tendril.

The imagery in this poem helps us picture the spider web in our minds. We can almost "see" the web. This poem uses words that create the feeling of sight. To identify imagery on the CRCT, look for words that describe something we experience with our five senses: Something we see, feel, taste, touch or hear. Let's practice.

Practice 1: Imagery

Answer the questions below. The first one has been done for you.

1. **Which of the following is the best example of imagery?**
    A. My feet sank into the soft, cool mud.
    B. The car drove quickly.
    C. The cookies were burnt.
    D. Sandra came over to listen to music.

Did you choose **A**? You're right! Option A describes how the mud feels when you step in it. It describes the sense of touch. The other options do not describe any of the five senses. Now, try a couple on your own.

2. **Which of the following is the weakest example of imagery?**

   A.   The chocolate ice cream tasted rich and creamy.

   B.   The sweater was soft and fuzzy against my skin.

   C.   The wind blew the leaves across the empty street, gathering in piles around lonely looking lampposts.

   D.   When it gets cold, the teachers won't let us go outside and play.

Read the poem below and answer the question.

Saturday Morning

Sleeping late

Waking up to

The whirr of lawn mowers

The whine of weed whackers

Children laughing

The clang of breakfast

Pots and pans in the kitchen

And later, with luck,

The lilting music of the ice cream truck.

3. **Which of the five senses does the poem above describe?**

   A.   Sight

   B.   Touch

   C.   Sound

   D.   Taste

4. **Try writing your own piece of prose or a poem using imagery. You can start by listing the five senses: sound, taste, touch, sight and smell. Under each category put words that describe one of these senses. For instance, under sound, you could put crickets: Under taste, lemons: Under smell, pine, etc. Use whatever sensory rich words you can think of. Then, use these words to create a poem or some sentences. Have fun with it and be creative!**

PERSONIFICATION — MAKING THINGS HUMAN

> We will answer the test questions: "Which of the following is an example of personification?" and "What is being personified in this poem or passage?"

When authors give human qualities to something not human, such as animals, objects or ideas, they use personification. Authors use **personification** to make things that are not human seem human. Here are a few examples: *The trees whispered and sighed. The sun smiled. The baby chicks cried. The cat frowned.* To identify personification, look for words that give human characteristics to something not human. If the question asks what is being personified in a passage, look for the thing, animal, object or idea that is given human characteristics. Let's practice.

Practice 2: Personification

Answer the questions below. The first one has been done for you.

1. **Which of the following is an example of personification?**
    A.   The sun was bright and hot.
    B.   The dog barked.
    C.   The birds flew.
    D.   The leaves danced in the wind.

If you chose **D**, you're right! The leaves are personified in this example. They are given the human ability to dance. Since the other options do not have any human characteristics, they are not examples of personification. Now try on your own.

2. **Which of the following is an example of personification?**
    A.   The cat hissed at Ronnie Reynolds.
    B.   The Earth shivered and sighed.
    C.   The candle flickered.
    D.   I watched the willow tree.

Two Sunflowers Move in the Yellow Room by William Blake

"Ah, William, we're weary of weather,"
Said the sunflowers, shining with dew.
"Our traveling habits have tired us.
Can you give us a room with a view?"

They arranged themselves at the window
And counted the steps of the sun,
And they both took root in the carpet
Where the topaz tortoises run.

3. **What is being personified in this poem?**

    A. a window

    B. the sun

    C. sunflowers

    D. the weather

4. **What human quality is given to something not human in this poem to make it person-ification?**

    A. The flowers are given the ability to speak.

    B. The sun is given the ability to write.

    C. The weather is given the ability to feel.

    D. The flowers are given the ability to draw.

SIMILE — COMPARING USING "LIKE" AND "AS"

> **We will answer the test question: "Which of the following is an example of simile?"**

A **simile** is a comparison of two unlike things, often using the words "like" or "as." **Examples:** *She's as pretty as a rose. He's as timid as a mouse. He eats like a pig. The snow was like a white sheet.* Identifying a simile is easy. Just look for comparisons and the words "like" and "as." For example, look at the following: "The clouds looked like cotton balls in the sky." What two things are being compared in this sentence? Clouds and cotton balls. How do we know it's a simile? It has the word "like." Now that you know what simile is, let's practice.

Practice 3: Simile

A.

Answer the questions below. The first one has been done for you.

1. **Which of the following is an example of a simile?**

   A. The dancers were as graceful as swans.

   B. The water was cold in the pool.

   C. The house was a mess.

   D. The mouse yawned.

If you chose **A**, you're right! We know it is a simile because there is
a comparison, dancers and swans, and the word "as." There are no comparisons in the other options
and the words "like" and "as" are absent. They are not similes. Option **A** is the best answer. Now
try on your own.

2. **Which of the following is NOT an example of simile?**

   A. The water was like glass.

   B. The cookies were hard as steel.

   C. The floor was wet.

   D. Her fingernails are thin as paper.

3. **Which of the following is an example of simile?**

   A. Katie grew like a weed.

   B. The fried chicken smelled delicious.

   C. Pizza is one of my favorite foods.

   D. The garden was fresh and green.

B.

Read the passage below. Each sentence has been numbered. Look for sentences with similes as you read. Then answer questions 4 through 7.

(**1**) Jacob turned the key in the ignition and started the tractor. (**2**) His father sat behind him, telling him what to do. (**3**) This was the first time Jacob would drive the tractor himself. (**4**) He was nervous — his heart beating like the fluttering of bird's wings against a steel cage. (**5**)"Now, put it into gear and slowly let off the brake," his father yelled over the loud rattling of the old engine. (**6**) Jacob did as he was told. (**7**) The large tractor moved forward, bouncing and bumping over the ground like a rickety carnival ride. (**8**) They came to the gates that opened up to the large pasture where they kept their horses. (**9**) The long grass swayed in the wind like waves on the surface of an ocean. (**10**) "All right, now," his father said, "you have to get off the tractor and open up the gates." (**11**) Jacob knew this was the hardest part of this job. (**12**) Trying to keep the horses from running through the gates while he opened them and drove the tractor through. (**13**) He could see Equinox, the fine black stallion his father had just bought, waiting near the gate. (**14**) Too close. (**15**) Equinox whinnied and tossed his head about like a wild beast ready to charge. (**16**) Jacob looked back at his father uncertainly. (**17**) "Throw a couple rocks his way," his father said matter-of-factly. "He'll move." (**18**) Jacob picked up a handful of rocks and tossed them lightly. (**19**) He didn't want to hurt the creature but scare it. (**20**) Before the rocks reached him, Equinox ran like lightning through the open gate over a softly rolling hill and disappeared.

4. **Which of the following sentences is an example of simile?**

    A.   Sentence number 1

    B.   Sentence number 13

    C.   Sentence number 19

    D.   Sentence number 4

5. **What is the tractor being compared to in sentence 7?**

    A.   a bird

    B.   a horse

    C.   a carnival ride

    D.   an old shoe

6. **What is Jacob's heartbeat compared to in sentence 4?**

   A. a wild beast

   B. the fluttering of bird's wings

   C. lightning

   D. a rabbit

7. **How many sentences in this passage have similes?**

   A. 5   B. 4   C. 6   D. 7

METAPHOR — COMPARING WITHOUT "LIKE" OR "AS"

> **We will answer the test question: "Which of the following is an example of metaphor?"**

A **metaphor** is comparing one thing to another *without* using the words "like" or "as." Although metaphor compares things like simile, it packs a bigger punch. Metaphor turns one thing into something else. Unlike simile, you are not "like" a chicken or scared "as" a chicken; you ARE a chicken. **Examples**: *Clouds are cotton candy. Mountains are giants. My fingers are icicles.* To identify metaphor, look for comparisons that turn one thing into something else. Remember, if you see the words "like" or "as," it is not a metaphor. It is a simile. Let's practice.

Practice 4:   Metaphor

Answer the questions below. The first one has been done for you.

1. **Which of the following sentences is an example of metaphor?**

   A. Michael was as strong as a horse.

   B. The ladybug danced at my window.

   C. My cat's a lion.

   D. Katherine moves like a stiff robot.

Did you choose **C**? You're right! The cat is being compared and turned into a lion. It is a metaphor. Options **A** and **D** are incorrect because they are similes. They both compare things using the word "as." Option **B** is incorrect because it is personification, not a metaphor. The ladybug is given the human quality of dance. Option **C** is the best answer. Now try a few on your own.

2. **Which of the following is an example of metaphor?**

    A.   The book was as heavy as a brick.

    B.   The ducks marched.

    C.   The wind screamed.

    D.   Every day is a new page in the book of life.

3. **Which of the following is a metaphor?**

    A.   It's as hot as an oven outside.

    B.   She looks like an angel.

    C.   Tom's a giant.

    D.   Kelly jumped as high as a deer.

4. **Which of the following is a metaphor?**

    A.   Eyes are windows to the soul.

    B.   Swim like a fish.

    C.   Sweet as honey on bread.

    D.   Mean as a snake.

HYPERBOLE — AN EXAGGERATION

> **We will answer the test question: "Which of the following is an example of hyperbole?"**

Hyperbole is used to add emphasis to what an author is trying to say. **Hyperbole** is an exaggeration or presenting something as larger or greater than it actually is. It is often used in poems and prose to add humor. **Examples**: *I'm starved. I died laughing. His nose was so big planes could have landed on it.*

Sometimes readers confuse hyperbole with simile and metaphor because it compares things. For example: "Her feet were as big as boats." Notice the word "as" is used, just like in a simile, to compare feet and boats. But it is an exaggeration. Boats can be hundreds of feet long. Someone's feet could never be that big! Just remember a **hyperbole** is an exaggeration, and you won't get confused.

Now that you know what hyperbole is, let's practice.

Practice 5: Hyperbole

Answer the questions below. The first one has been done for you.

1. Which of the following is an example of hyperbole?

  A. My mouth was on fire after I ate the hot pepper.

  B. My dad is a sturdy mountain.

  C. Sandy looked white as a ghost.

  D. Robert was as patient as a saint.

If you chose **A**, you're right! Eating hot peppers will never really set your mouth on fire (although it may feel like it). This statement is an exaggeration. Options **C** and **D** are incorrect because they are similes. Option **B** is incorrect because it is an example of metaphor, not hyperbole. Now try a couple on your own.

2. Which of the following is an example of hyperbole?

  A. The water was clear as crystal.

  B. Carla was a kitten.

  C. The rain fell like teardrops from heaven.

  D. Corey's grandmother is as old as dirt.

3. Which of the following is NOT an example of hyperbole?

  A. I'm so hungry I could eat a horse.

  B. I've tried a thousand times.

  C. My teacher's so old her name is in my history book.

  D. The monkeys climbed and swung from the trees like gymnasts.

4. Which of the following is an example of hyperbole?

  A. The mountains stretched their heads to the sky.

  B. I waited an eternity for my dad to pick me up.

  C. Our toy boat sank like a stone in the water.

  D. The storm was a monster.

CHAPTER 4 SUMMARY

Figurative language — using words in a way that means more than the dictionary definition. Figurative language doesn't mean exactly what it says. We learned about five different kinds of figurative language in this chapter: *Imagery, personification, simile, metaphor and hyperbole.*

- **Imagery** — describing what we experience with our five senses. Imagery creates the feeling of sight, touch, hearing, smell or taste.

- **Personification** — giving human qualities to something not human. Authors use personification to make things inhuman seem human.

- **Simile** — a comparison of two things, often using the words "like" or "as."

- **Metaphor** — comparing one thing to another *without* using the words "like" or "as."

- **Hyperbole** — an exaggeration. An exaggeration is an overstatement or presenting something as larger or greater than it actually is.

CHAPTER 4 REVIEW

Read the sentences and passages below. Then answer the questions.

> "As the workmen began to clear another forest, the Earth sighed sadly and began to cry."

1. The sentence above is an example of

A. hyperbole.

B. metaphor.

C. simile.

D. personification.

> "I was so surprised you could've knocked me over with a feather."

2. This sentence above is an example of

A. hyperbole.

B. personification.

C. imagery.

D. metaphor.

> "The candle was like the sun sweeping the darkness away."

3. This sentence above is an example of

A. metaphor.

B. simile.

C. refrain.

D. personification.

> "He's a turkey."

4. This sentence is an example of

A. metaphor.

B. imagery.

C. hyperbole.

D. refrain.

The Great Figure

by William Carlos Williams

AMONG the rain

and lights

I saw the figure 5

in gold

on a red

firetruck

moving tense

unheeded

to gong clangs

siren howls

and wheels rumbling

through the dark city.

5. What type of figurative language is used in this poem?

A. metaphor

B. hyperbole

C. imagery

D. simile

6. What is being described in this poem?

A. an ambulance

B. a colorful rain

C. a lighthouse

D. a fire truck

"You're acting like a monkey."

7. What type of figurative language is used in this sentence?

A. hyperbole

B. simile

C. metaphor

D. imagery

"You are a monkey."

8. What type of figurative language is used in this sentence?

A. metaphor

B. simile

C. personification

D. imagery

"Winter reached out his withered hand and sprinkled snow across the land."

9. The sentence above is an example of what kind of figurative language?

A. iImagery

B. hyperbole

C. metaphor

D. personification

"The elephant's ears are so big if he flapped them he'd fly."

10. **The sentence above is an example of what kind of figurative language?**

    A. personification

    B. hyperbole

    C. simile

    D. metaphor

"This room is a pigsty!"

11. **The sentence above is an example of what kind of figurative language?**

    A. hyperbole

    B. simile

    C. metaphor

    D. imagery

"At night, the attic was like a large and mysterious cave."

12. **What type of figurative language is used in this sentence?**

    A. metaphor

    B. personification

    C. hyperbole

    D. simile

Chapter 5
Vocabulary

This chapter covers GeorgiasStandard(s)

ELA5R1-B	understand and apply knowledge of glossary
ELA5R3-B	understand and determine the meaning of unfamiliar words by using context clues
ELA5R3-C & ELA5R3-E	determine the meaning of common prefixes, suffixes, and roots
ELA5R3-H	comprehend and use words with multiple meanings to determine which meaning is intended from the context
ELA5R3-I	apply the meaning of terms, such as antonym, synonym, and homophone

 On the CRCT, you will be asked questions about **word meaning** (vocabulary). You may see words you don't understand. Don't worry. You're not alone. Since there are millions of words, even the most well-read person doesn't know the meaning of every one of them.

Ideally, you should look up words you don't know in the dictionary. Sometimes this isn't possible, especially in a testing situation. But you can figure out the meaning of unfamiliar words, without using a dictionary, in a number of tried and true ways. We will go over a few of those ways in this chapter.

CONTEXT CLUES — THE WORDS AROUND THE WORD

> We will answer the test question: "What does the word _____ mean in this passage?"

Vocabulary

One of the best ways to learn the meaning of new words is to look at **context clues**. Context clues give you hints about the meaning of a new word through the words or sentences around it. For example:

> "The long hike was too <u>arduous</u>. I had to stop and catch my breath before going on."

The words around the word "arduous" are the context clues. Even if you're not sure what "arduous" means, you can figure it out by looking at the other words or sentences around it. We know from the first sentence that the author is hiking. We know from the second sentence that the author is tired and has to stop and rest. Based on these clues, we can correctly guess that the word "arduous" means hard or difficult. When you're not sure what a word means, look at the words around the unknown word for clues.

There are four kinds of context clues commonly used in passages. Below is a list of them. Look for key words, sometimes called **signal words,** that may help you figure out the meaning of new words.

Definition and Restatement Context Clues	The meaning of the unknown word is defined or restated in the sentence or passage. Look for key words such as *is, is called, that is, or, is defined as, means, who is, that is, in other words, which.*

Examples:

An **etymologist**, *or* a **bug expert**, studies many kinds of insects.

An **optimist** *is* someone who remains **positive** even in the worst situations.

Contrast Context Clues

The unknown word has the opposite meaning of a familiar word or words in a passage. Key words to look for: *but, however, not, while, yet, on the other hand, instead of, unlike, although, the opposite of.*

Examples:

My older brother told me my 5th grade teacher, Ms. Stone, was a **tyrant**. *However*, I think she's **nice**.

Steven is usually very **boisterous** *while* his sister is very **quiet** and **shy**.

Comparison Context Clues

The unknown word has the same meaning as a familiar word or words in a passage. Key words to look for: *like, as, in the same way, both, is similar, also, and.*

Examples:

My mom said the mountains were very **tranquil**; I *also* thought they were **peaceful**.

The **tome** weighed a ton, *and* I had to carry the heavy **book** all the way home.

Example Context Clues

The meaning of an unknown word is explained in an example in the sentence or passage. Key words: *for example, for instance, such as.*

Examples:

People use all kinds of **vehicles** *such as* **cars**, **bicycles**, **scooters** and **motorcycles**.

There are many kinds of **legumes** you can use to make soup. *For instance*, you can use **black**, **white**, **navy** or **kidney beans** in your soup.

Vocabulary

Practice 1:   Context Clues

Read the sentences below and answer the questions. The first one has been done for you.

1. **I *hesitated* before I jumped off the diving board. The pool below looked so far away. It was a little scary. I had to take a moment to work up the nerve to jump.**

    What does the word **hesitated** mean?

    A.   paused

    B.   looked

    C.   ran

    D.   jumped

Did you choose **A**? You're right! The other sentences in the passage give us clues to the meaning. The first and second sentences say the pool was far away and the author is scared. The last sentence says that the author had to take a moment before jumping. With these clues, we can correctly guess that hesitated means to pause. Now try a few on your own.

2. **The air was *frigid* outside, and the thermometer said it was twenty-two degrees.**

    The word **frigid** means

    A.   clean.

    B.   cold.

    C.   hot.

    D.   dirty.

3. **Sally was very *gregarious*. She always smiled and talked to everyone. No wonder she was so popular.**

    Gregarious means

    A.   outgoing.

    B.   sad.

    C.   scared.

    D.   stuck-up.

4. **The thought of eating bugs is *appalling* to most people, but in some countries eating insects is considered a treat.**

   What does **appalling** mean?

   A. enjoyable

   B. difficult

   C. disgusting

   D. different

5. **There were several *confections* on the table such as chocolate chip cookies, three chocolate cakes and four apple pies.**

   What are **confections**?

   A. sweet desserts

   B. sandwiches

   C. cakes

   D. fruit and cheese

6. **The mountain climber reached the *apex* of the mountain. He put a flag in the ground which marked the highest point before he began his climb back down.**

   Apex most likely means

   A. valley.

   B. hill.

   C. to climb.

   D. the top.

7. **Michael's room was always *immaculate*. However, his sister's room was always a mess.**

   What does the word **immaculate** mean?

   A. clean and tidy

   B. filthy and dirty

   C. large and empty

   D. small and cluttered

8. Our *meager* meal was only a few crumbs of bread, not even enough for a mouse.

The word **meager** means

A.   plenty.

B.   large.

C.   delicious.

D.   small.

WORDS WITH MULTIPLE MEANINGS — WHAT'S MY MEANING?.

> We will answer the test question: "What does the word _____ mean in this sentence?"

As we just learned, context clues can help you figure out the meaning of new words. But what about words that have more than one meaning? Context clues are usually the only way to figure out which meaning is meant in a word that has **multiple meanings**. For instance, take the word "address." If we just look at the word, without a context, it could mean a couple of different things: It could mean your home address, to speak or discuss a problem, or a speech by an important person. It is only when we look at context clues that the

meaning becomes clear. For example, "The teacher *addressed* me in a quiet voice." The meaning of "address" in this sentence is how someone speaks or talks. Context clues help you figure out which meaning is meant. Now that we know how to use context clues to figure out the meaning of new words, let's look at words that have more than one meaning. Let's practice.

Practice 2:   Words with Multiple Meanings

Using the list of words below, choose the right word to correctly complete each sentence. **Hint:** Each word is used twice. The first one has been done for you.

bat	race	sink
lean	rose	snap

1.   When Kelsey got sleepy, she would _____ her head on her father's shoulder.

Did you choose **lean**? You got it! The key word here is "sleepy." Now try the rest on your own.

2. After working out a lot, Johnathan became _____ and strong.

3. Cody held the _____ firmly, waiting for the pitch.

4. I watched my cat _____ at the butterfly that flew past.

5. After we ate dinner, I put the dishes in the _____.

6. The ship began to _____ into the ocean.

7. Matthew ran as fast as he could to win the _____.

8. Shelley watched the cars _____ around the track.

9. I was afraid the rubber band would _____ if I stretched it too much.

10. You should never make a _____ decision about important things.

11. Sarah gave her mother a beautiful red _____ for her birthday.

12. The sun _____ bright and cheery over the horizon.

ROOTS, PREFIXES, AND SUFFIXES — BREAKING DOWN WORDS

> We will answer the test questions: "Which of the following words has a prefix that means *two* or *twice*?" or "Which of the following words has a suffix that means *full of*?"

Learning about **roots, prefixes** and **suffixes** is another way to understand new words. A word can be broken down into parts. These parts are called the root, prefix and suffix. The first part of a word is the **prefix**. The main part of a word is the **root**. The last part of a word is the **suffix**. For example, look at the word **dishonestly: dis** is the prefix, **honest** is the root, and **ly** is the suffix. Learning the meanings of certain roots, prefixes and suffixes will help you understand new words.

Root	The main part of a word is the root. Here are a few root words and their meanings.
annu and anni	year **Examples:** *annu*al, *anni*versary.
deca	ten **Example:** *deca*de
phon	sound **Example:** tele*phon*e
path	feeling **Examples:** *path*etic, sym*path*ize
aqua	water **Example:** *aqua*rium
multi	many **Example:** *multi*ply
bio	life **Example:** *bio*logy
dict	to say or speak **Examples:** *Dict*ator, ver*dict*

Prefix	The prefix is at the beginning of a word. Prefixes are always attached to a root word. Here are a few common prefixes and their meanings.
bi	two or twice **Examples:** *bi*-annual (every two years), *bi*lingual (someone who speaks two languages) and *bi*cycle (a bike with two wheels).
tri	three **Examples:** *tri*cycle (bike with three wheels), and *tri*plets (three babies).
un, in, im, and il	not **Examples:** When you're not able, you're *un*able. Something not possible is *im*possible. Something not legal is *ill*egal. Something not formal is *in*formal.
dis	to take away, the opposite of **Example:** When you take away respect, it's *dis*respect. When you leave school for home, you are *dis*missed
mis	wrong or badly **Examples:** *mis*behave, *mis*inform, *mis*take.
pre	something that comes before **Examples:** *pre*fix, *pre*pare, *pre*view.
re	to do again **Examples:** *re*view, *re*read, *re*play.

Suffix	The suffix is at the end of a word. Suffixes are always attached to a root word. Here are a few common suffixes and their meanings.
er	someone who does something or whose job it is **Examples:** A person who runs is a runn*er*. Someone who bakes is a bak*er*. Someone who gardens is a garden*er*.
able	capable of being **Examples:** a person who is easy to get along with is agree*able* or like*able*. Someone we care about is ador*able* or lovable.
ous	full of or having **Examples:** A house that has a lot of room is spac*ious*. Someone who is full of kindness is grac*ious*.
ness	state of or quality **Examples:** restless*ness*, kind*ness*.
less	without **Example:** someone without fear is fear*less*.
ful	full of **Examples:** cheer*ful*, plenti*ful*, fright*ful*, help*ful*, care*ful*.
ly	like, in the manner of **Examples:** quiet*ly*, easi*ly*, hopeless*ly*.
ment	an act or instance of doing something or a state of being **Examples:** entertain*ment*, amaze*ment*, content*ment*.

Chapter 5

Practice 3: Roots, Prefixes, and Suffixes

Read the following questions and choose the best answer. The first two have been done for you.

1. What does the "*re*" in repeat mean?

   A. full of

   B. not

   C. to do again

   D. before

Did you choose **C**? You got it! The prefix "re" means to do again. Let's try another one for practice.

2. Which of the following words has a suffix that means *full of*?

   A. delightful

   B. capable

   C. enjoyment

   D. painter

If you chose **A**, you're right again! The suffix "ful" in the word delightful means full of. Now try a few on your own.

3. Which of the following words contains a prefix that means *wrongly or badly*?

   A. misguided

   B. unafraid

   C. dislike

   D. preschool

4. What prefix would you add to the word "acceptable" to make it mean "not acceptable?"

   A. dis   C. mis

   B. pre   D. un

5. A suffix is always

   A. in the middle of the word.

   B. at the beginning of the word.

   C. at the end of the word.

   D. outside of the word.

6. **Which of the following suffixes means *someone who does something*?**

   A. able

   B. er

   C. ous

   D. ly

7. **Which of the following words has a prefix that means *three*?**

   A. tricolor

   B. unclean

   C. invisible

   D. friendly

8. **Which of the following words has a suffix that means *like or in the manner of*?**

   A. joyfully

   B. nervous

   C. excitement

   D. carelessness

9. **What does the root "phon" in megaphone mean?**

   A. silent

   B. ten

   C. three

   D. sound

10. **What does the root word "multi" mean?**

   A. complex

   B. full of

   C. many

   D. capable of

ANTONYM, SYNONYM, AND HOMOPHONE

> **We will answer the test questions: "Which of the following is an antonym or homophone?"** *and* **"What word is a synonym for jump?"**

Another way to improve your vocabulary skills is learning about **synonyms**, **antonyms** and **homophones**. Learning about these word skills will help you increase your score on the CRCT.

Synonyms are words that have the same or almost the same meaning.

> **Example:** *Large* is a synonym for *big*. *Little* is a synonym for *tiny*. *Giggle* is a synonym for *laugh*. *Jump* is a synonym for *leap*.

Antonyms are words that have opposite meaning.

> **Example:** *Hot* is an antonym for *cold*. *Tall* is an antonym for *short*. *Day* is an antonym for *night*.

Homophones are words that sound the same but have different meanings and usually different spellings.

> **Example:** *meet* and *meat*; *heard* and *herd*; *there* and *their*.

Practice 4: Synonyms, Antonyms, and Homophones

Read the sentences and passages below. Then circle the best answer. The first one has been done for you.

1. **Which word is an antonym of** *sadly*?

    A. madly

    B. sorrowfully

    C. happily

    D. lonely

If you chose **C**, you're right! Happily is the opposite of sadly. They are antonyms. Now try a few on your own.

Sam looked at his dinner plate sadly. Everything was gone except for eight dreaded brussel sprouts. He knew he wouldn't be able to go to Chase's house if he didn't eat them. Sam held his nose, opened his mouth, and ate the disgusting brussel sprouts.

2. The words *ate* and *eight* are

   A. synonyms.

   B. antonyms.

   C. homophones.

   D. nouns.

3. Which word is a synonym for *disgusting*?

   A. gross

   B. delicious

   C. appealing

   D. delightful

We were driving home from camp. It was dark, and the roads were wet. My dear mom drove carefully. Suddenly, a large deer ran out into the road — right in front of us! My mom slammed on the brakes, and we slid sideways on the road. When we stopped, I looked up to see the deer running away from the road unharmed.

4. Which word is an antonym of *wet*?

   A. dry

   B. slick

   C. wet

   D. slimy

5. Which word is a synonym of *carefully*?

   A. carelessly

   B. safely

   C. dangerously

   D. bravely

6. *Deer* and *dear* are

   A. adjectives.

   B. synonyms.

   C. antonyms.

   D. homophones.

7. **Which word is an antonym of *stopped*?**

   A. halted

   B. ended

   C. paused

   D. moved

8. **Which word is a synonym of *unharmed*?**

   A. wounded

   B. unhurt

   C. injured

   D. hurt

For questions nine through twelve, choose the right homophone to complete the sentence.

9. **The cut on my hand will_____.**

   A. heel

   B. heal

10. **The apple trees _____ a lot of fruit in the fall.**

   A. bare

   B. bear

11. **My little brother is turning _____ next week.**

   A. for

   B. four

12. **The captain told us to _____ the ship.**

   A. board

   B. bored

USING A GLOSSARY — LOOKING IT UP!

> We will answer the test question: "What does the word _____ mean in this glossary?"

At the end of some books and stories, you will sometimes find a glossary. It is like a dictionary but much shorter. A **glossary** is an alphabetical list of words and their meanings. You should use it to learn new words when you can. Studying new words will help you do better on the CRCT and will help you become a better reader.

Practice 5: Glossary

Sample Glossary Page

anonymous	with no name known
apparition	a ghost
assortment	a group or collection of different items
avarice	greed for riches
belligerent	aggressive and eager to fight
bustle	to move quickly and busily
cantankerous	ill-tempered or bad tempered
consolation	something that makes someone feel better

Using the information above, answer the following questions.

1. **Someone who is cantankerous is**

   A. nice and polite.

   B. mean and bad tempered.

   C. enthusiastic and spry.

   D. slow and lazy.

2. **Which word means to move quickly or busily?**

    A.   belligerent

    B.   assortment

    C.   avarice

    D.   bustle

3. **Which word means a group or collection of items?**

    A.   apparition

    B.   anonymous

    C.   assortment

    D.   consolation

4. **An anonymous author is a writer**

    A.   with several names.

    B.   without a name.

    C.   with a name.

    D.   with a familiar name.

5. **Someone who is anxious to fight is**

    A.   belligerent.

    B.   anonymous.

    C.   cantankerous.

    D.   generous.

CHAPTER 5 SUMMARY

Context clues — hints about the meaning of a new word through the words or sentences around an unknown word. We covered four kinds of context clues in this chapter.

- **Definition and Restatement Context Clues** — The meaning of the unknown word is defined or restated in the sentence or passage.

- **Contrast Context Clues** — The meaning of the unknown word is the opposite of a familiar word or words in a passage.

- **Comparison Context Clues** — The meaning of the unknown word is the same as a familiar word or words in a passage.

- **Example Context Clues** — The meaning of an unknown word is explained in an example in the sentence or passage.

Multiple Meanings — Multiple meaning words have more than one meaning.

Root — The main part of a word is the root.

Prefix — The prefix is at the beginning of a word. Prefixes are always attached to a root word.

Suffix — The suffix is at the end of a word. Suffixes are always attached to a root word.

Synonyms — Synonyms are words that have the same or almost the same meaning.

Antonyms — Antonyms are words that have opposite meaning.

Homophones — Homophones are words that sound the same but have different meanings and usually different spellings.

Glossary — The glossary is an alphabetical list of words and their meanings found at the end of a book or story.

CHAPTER 5 REVIEW

Read the sentences below and answer the questions.

> Mr. Carver does not *tolerate* or permit talking in the classroom.

1. **What does the word tolerate mean in this sentence?**

    A. allow

    B. hear

    C. stop

    D. homework

> We were able to *apprehend* the thief after years of trying to catch him.

2. **What does the word apprehend mean?**

    A. help

    B. see

    C. capture

    D. trick

> Don't *distract* Kelly when she's trying to study. In other words, be quiet and don't make a lot of noise.

3. **What does the word distract mean?**

    A. ignore

    B. telephone

    C. question

    D. disturb

> Sarah had a sore throat. Her voice was so low it was almost *inaudible*. We could barely hear what she was trying to say to us.

4. **What does inaudible mean?**

   A. annoying

   B. hard to hear

   C. talking loudly

   D. food that is not edible

> Steven turned *abruptly*. He moved so quickly he almost bumped into the principal.

5. **What does the word abruptly mean?**

   A. fast and sudden

   B. slow and clumsy

   C. quiet and sneaky

   D. polite and proper

6. **Sally climbed the _____ quickly. She wanted to make it up to her room before her little sister did.**

   A. stares

   B. stairs

7. **Megan gave me directions to her house. We have to take a _____ into her neighborhood.**

   A. right

   B. write

8. **Paper is made out of _____.**

   A. would

   B. wood

9. Henry _____ the ball so hard it hurt my hand when I caught it.

    A. through

    B. threw

10. Precooked chicken is chicken that's been cooked _____ you buy it.

    A. after

    B. before

11. What suffix added to the word home means someone *without* a home?

    A. ness

    B. er

    C. less

    D. ly

12. If the root word dict means to speak, what book tells you the meaning and pronunciation of words?

    A. encyclopedia

    B. dictionary

    C. textbook

    D. novel

13. What word means the same thing as solution?

    A. question

    B. answer

    C. problem

    D. puzzle

14. Which word means the opposite of hungry?

    A. starving

    B. empty

    C. famished

    D. full

Chapter 6
Media

This chapter covers Georgia standard(s)

ELA5LSV2	demonstrates an awareness of the media in the daily lives of most people
	judges the extent to which media provides a source of entertainment as well as a source of information
	evaluates the role of the media in focusing attention and in forming an opinion

Did you know that you see and hear hundreds of messages every day? These messages come through **media** to influence people. Television, radio, the Internet, video games, newspapers, books and magazines are all forms of media. They all have a purpose. Some media inform or teach, and others entertain or persuade people to do or not do something. On the CRCT, you will be asked to read different kinds of media and to **evaluate** (judge) media messages.

In this chapter, we will learn how to evaluate certain media messages, such as advertisements. We will also discuss how media is part of everyday life and how media is a source of information as well as entertainment.

Learning more about media will give you the skills to make better decisions about what you buy or ask your parents to buy. Get ready — we're going to "tune in" to the world of media.

MEDIA IN DAILY LIFE — HOW PLUGGED IN ARE WE?

> **In this section, we will answer the question: "How is media part of everyday life?"**

How much time do you think you spend in front of the television or on the computer each day? An hour? Maybe two? According to experts, probably much more than that. If you're the average kid, you probably spend four or more hours a day watching television. If you don't watch television, how often do you hear the radio? Listen to a CD? Read a magazine? Or play video games? These are all forms of media, and we are exposed to it every day. It is almost impossible to avoid. It is everywhere: On billboards, commercials and even in the school lunchroom (got milk?) We encounter media so often, we may not even be aware of how much it is part of everyday life.

Practice 1: Media in Everyday Life

To find out just how big a role media plays in daily life, track how much television you watch each day for a week. On a blank sheet of paper, write down the time you started watching and the names of the shows you watch. Then answer the following questions:

1. **How many hours of television did I watch each day?**

2. **What did I like most about watching television?**

3. **What did I like least about watching television?**

4. **How did I feel after watching television?**

5. **What is my favorite program?**

6. **What is my least favorite program?**

7. **Did I learn anything watching television?**

8. **Did I use my television as background noise?**

This practice should give you a better understanding of your own media habits. It should also give you a better idea of how much media you are exposed to every day. You might be surprised by what you discover.

MEDIA'S PURPOSE — ENTERTAIN AND INFORM

> In this section, we will answer the question: "What is the purpose of this type of media?"

In Chapter 1, we learned about author's purpose. Media also has a purpose. The two main purposes of media are to **inform** and to **entertain**. Media that entertains includes major movies, video games, CDs, DVDs, some television programs and entertainment magazines. Media that informs includes educational television programs, CDs, DVDs, magazines, books, journals and Web sites.

At times, media can do both at the same time. For example, a television show about whales can be entertaining as well as informational. When something is entertaining, we usually pay more attention. When we pay more attention, we learn more. This is why you watch certain films in school or read certain magazines like *Time for Kids*. The purpose is to teach and entertain at the same time.

Practice 2:   Media's Purpose

Read the following sentences. Decide whether the purpose is to entertain, inform or both. The first one has been done for you.

1. **A new movie about a race car driver trying to win the race of a lifetime is coming out this weekend. The purpose of this movie is to**

   A.   inform or teach.

   B.   entertain.

Did you choose **B**? You're right! Most movies are only meant to entertain. Now, try a few on your own.

2. **A television show about the solar system and scientists' new discoveries is on tonight at 8:00 pm. The purpose of this show is to**

   A.   entertain.

   B.   inform.

3. **The purpose of a Web site about endangered animals in Africa is to**

   A.   inform.

   B.   entertain.

4. **The main purpose of a new hip-hop CD by Cindy Swell is to**

   A. inform.

   B. entertain.

5. **The purpose of a morning radio show that plays music and news is to**

   A. inform and entertain.

   B. entertain.

USING MEDIA TO FIND INFORMATION — WHERE TO LOOK?

> **In this section, we will answer the question: "Where is the BEST place to look to find information on _____ ?"**

Media can be a good **source of information**. With more media than ever before, we now have more information than ever before. You can get information on just about anything anytime you'd like.

With all the information the media provides, it can be difficult to know where to look to find the information you need. For example, imagine you are doing a report on hurricanes. You will find a lot of different information on hurricanes in the media. A newspaper may have articles about hurricane Katrina. The Internet site may talk about how hurricanes are tracked. The local news on television may show pictures of the destruction a hurricane causes.

Your first step is to figure out what you need to know. Once you know this, you'll have a better idea what type of media will give you the best information.
Following is a list of some different kinds of media and the kind of information each one usually gives.

Newspaper	A newspaper is a printed publication that contains information about current events and local happenings, such as fairs or festivals. A newspaper can include sections on business, political events, the arts, crime, weather forecasts, advertisements and **editorials** (articles that express an opinion or attitude about a local or national issue).
Television	Television is an electronic form of media mainly used to entertain. Television programs range from news, sports, dramas, comedies, movies, talk shows, advertisements and much more. Some television programs can also be used to educate or inform people, such as *Sesame Street*.
Magazines	Magazines contain articles and many advertisements. You can find different magazines on a number of topics, including beauty, health, sports, fishing, cars, etc. Different kinds of magazines offer different kinds of information. You wouldn't look, for example, in a beauty magazine to find out about NASCAR.
The Internet	Every type of media discussed above can be found on the Internet. You can access newspapers, magazines and Web sites online. You can even watch television. The Internet is an invaluable tool to use. It is usually the first place people go to look for information.

Practice 3: Using Media to Find Information

Read the following passages. Then answer the questions. The first one has been done for you.

1. **Matthew is making a model of a volcano for a science project. Where would be the BEST place to look to find out how to make a model?**
   A. a newspaper article about volcanoes in Hawaii
   B. a radio program about the history of destructive volcanoes
   C. a magazine that has a picture of a volcano
   D. a Web site on how to make a volcano

Did you choose **D**? You're right! The best place to look would be a Web site on how to make a volcano. The other options had different information about volcanoes. They did not have the information Matthew needed to build the model. Now, try a few on your own.

2. **Latisha needs to bring an example of a current event to her social studies class. Where would be the BEST place to look for one?**

    A. a newspaper

    B. a sports magazine

    C. a cooking show on television

    D. a radio program about places to visit in Georgia

3. **Melanie is looking for information on new styles and trends in fashion for girls. Where would be the BEST place to look?**

    A. a newspaper

    B. a hobby magazine

    C. a beauty magazine

    D. a home and garden magazine

4. **Robert is having a hard time understanding math. Where would be the BEST place to look for help?**

    A. a science magazine

    B. an article about math tests in a newspaper

    C. a Web site that offers tutoring in math

    D. a Web site that offers help with English

MEDIA MESSAGES — ADVERTISEMENTS

> In this section, we will answer the question: "What is an advertisement?"

As we just learned, media is a source of information and a source of entertainment. Media is also full of persuasive messages. These messages are called **advertisements**. You can find advertisements in newspapers, on television, on the Internet, in magazines, on the radio and in flyers.

An **advertisement** is designed to get your attention to sell you something — a product, an idea or even a person (for instance, someone who wants you to vote for him for class president).

Advertisements can be tricky. The people who make advertisements spend much time trying to make whatever they're selling look "cool" to you. They dress up their product, put it under bright lights, and make it look as irresistible as they can. They make impossible promises about how much "cooler" or "prettier" you will be if you buy whatever they're selling.

So, how do you avoid becoming a victim of advertising tricks? The first step is to **analyze** (or break down) what you see and hear in advertisements. We will learn about a few advertising tricks. Once you learn them, you'll be able to make better decisions about what you buy, from toys to the food you eat.

FINDING FACTS AND OPINIONS IN ADVERTISEMENTS

Many times advertisers will twist the truth or make something sound better than it actually is. Much of what you see and hear in the media is a mix of fact and opinion. There is nothing wrong with mixing fact and opinion together — it is done all the time. However, it is important to be able to distinguish a fact from opinion when you see or hear an advertisement. For example, look at the advertisement on the following page.

ATLANTA'S LEADING BICYCLE SUPPLIER

Located North of Atlanta at The Mall of Georgia

Over 800 New Models in Stock

Classes on Personal Bike Repair

Quality and Affordable Bike Parts

Operated by the Best Bike Experts

Atlanta's Largest Staffed Bike Shop

Can you find the opinion in this ad? If you think it's "Operated by the best bike experts," you're right! Knowing the difference between a fact and an opinion in an advertisement will help you make better decisions about what you buy.

A **fact** is a true statement that can be proven by observation or research.

An **opinion** is an attitude or viewpoint about something that cannot be proven true or false. Opinions sometimes include key phrases such as *I feel*, *I think* and *in my opinion*. They can also include words like *best*, *worst*, *favorite*, *number one*, etc.

Practice 4: Facts and Opinions in Advertisements

Look at the following advertisement. Then answer the questions that follow.

Benny's Pizza

The Best Pizza in Town!!

The Best Service in Town!!

Owned and Operated by the Barbera family for over 30 years.

Pizza dough made fresh daily.

Open Monday through Sunday 11:00 am to 10:00 pm.

---

1. **Which of the following is an opinion?**

    A.   Open Monday through Sunday 11:00 am to 10:00 pm.

    B.   Owned and Operated by the Barbera family for over 30 years.

    C.   The Best Pizza in town!!

    D.   Pizza dough made fresh daily.

2. **How many opinions are there in this advertisement?**

    A. 2   B. 1   C. 3   D. 7

3. **Which of the following is a fact?**

    A.   The Best Pizza in town!!

    B.   The Best Service in Town!!

    C.   Owned and Operated by the Barbera family for over 30 years.

    D.   There are no facts in this advertisement.

PERSUASION — HOW DO THEY SELL IT?

Persuasion is an attempt to form or change a person's opinion about something. Advertisements use persuasion to get you to buy products. Listed below are examples of some persuasive techniques used in advertising.

Bandwagon

An appeal to follow the crowd. Advertisers use bandwagon to make viewers or readers feel that if they don't join in, they will be left out or behind.

> **Example:** "No one uses dial-up Internet anymore, unless you're a caveman! So, get with it and get high speed DSL!"

Generalization

What is true for *one* person, is true for *all* people.

Example: "Bobbie made $500.00 selling baseball cards. If he can, you can!"

Scare Tactics

An advertisement that tries to scare you into buying products.

> **Example:** "If you don't eat our vitamins, your teeth will turn yellow, and your hair will fall out."

Testimonials

Advertisements that show famous people using or praising the product.

> **Example:** Britney Spears dancing and singing in a cola commercial.

Exaggeration

An advertisement that makes ridiculous claims or makes the product seem bigger or better than it really is.

> **Example:** "Buy Extreme skates, and you'll fly!"

All of these persuasive techniques are used to get you to buy what advertisers are selling. When you see an advertisement, look for these types of persuasion.

Practice 5: Identifying Persuasive Techniques in Advertisements

Study the following advertisements. Then answer the questions that follow them.

Want more friends?

Want to be popular?

Want to look gorgeous?

Then buy Lip-Stix. You'll get a new life.

1. **What type of persuasion is used in the ad above?**
    A.   The ad uses bandwagon.
    B.   The ad uses a testimonial.
    C.   The ad exaggerates.
    D.   The ad tries to scare readers.

2. **Which of the following does the ad promise if a teenager buys Lip-Stix?**

   A. boyfriends

   B. popularity

   C. money

   D. fame

3. **Do you think Lip-Stix can really give everything it promises? Why or why not?**

4. **Would this ad convince a teenager to try Lip-Stix?**

Noah Bird, the all-star Extreme Bike Stunts champion, always wears Shock-Proof brand helmets when he rides. "It's the best bike helmet out there. Trust me, *I know*. Buy a Shock-Proof helmet today, and shock your friends!"

---

5. **What kind of product is being advertised in this ad?**

   A. a skateboard

   B. a bike

   C. knee pads

   D. a helmet

6. **What type of persuasion is used in this ad?**

   A. The ad exaggerates.

   B. The ad uses bandwagon.

   C. The ad uses testimonial.

   D. The ad generalizes.

7. **If everyone else started buying it, would you want this product more? What if you knew there was a better brand out there? Would it change your opinion? Why or why not?**

SHOULD YOU BUY IT? READING THE FINE PRINT

A good rule of thumb to follow when you see an ad is, "If it sounds too good to be true, it usually is." Sometimes you have to look closely at an ad to figure out if it's a good deal. For example, look at the ad on the following page.

SALE!! SALE!   **HUGE SHOE SALE!!**

BUY ONE PAIR, GET SECOND PAIR FREE!!

Second pair has to be from the discontinued rack, only in size seven.

Offer applies only to sandals.

Not available at the mall.

To figure out if this deal is as good as it sounds, you have to read the **fine print**. The **fine print** is the tiny writing at the bottom of an ad that tells you the details of the offer. When we look at the fine print in the ad above, what is the first thing we notice? The sale only includes shoes that have been discontinued in a size seven. If you wear a seven, it might not be bad. But, let's look at the second line. The offer is only good on sandals. That narrows it down even more. The last line says the offer isn't available at the mall. If the mall is the closest shopping center to you, you may have to drive a bit to find this store and take advantage of the deal. Overall, the deal isn't bad *IF* you're looking for discontinued sandals in a size seven at a store other than the mall. If not, the deal isn't worth the trip.

It is also important to remember to read the fine print when you go to the grocery store or the toy store. The fine print on grocery store items can be found on the label in the list of ingredients and nutrition information. For toys, the fine print is usually on the back of the box.

Practice 6: Should you Buy it?

Look carefully at the following advertisements. Then, answer the questions below. Remember to read the fine print.

Includes one Cindy Lou doll.
Accessories sold separately.

1. **If you bought this, what would you find inside the box?**

    A.   the Cindy Lou doll with everything else on the front of the box

    B.   the Cindy Lou doll only

    C.   a high chair

    D.   Cindy Lou baby doll clothes

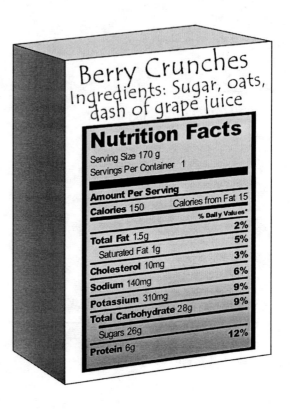

2. **What kind of berries are in this cereal?**

   A. blueberries

   B. strawberries

   C. boysenberries

   D. there are no berries

3. **How much sugar is in this cereal?**
   A. 140g   B. 26g   C. 28g   D. 6 mg

4. **Do you think this cereal is a healthy food choice? Why or why not?**

CHAPTER 6 SUMMARY

Media — any visual, audio or printed information that carries a message is called media. This includes television, radio, the Internet, video games, newspapers and magazines, DVDs and CDs.

Media's Purpose — media can be used to entertain, inform or entertain and inform.

Media as a Source of Information — In this chapter, we covered four kinds of media and the information they provide:

- **Newspaper** — a printed publication that contains information about current events and local happenings, such as festivals, meetings and movies.

- **Television** — an electronic form of media mainly used to entertain. Some television programs can educate and inform, such as *Sesame Street* and Discovery Channel.

- **Magazines** — you can find different magazines on a number of topics, including magazines on beauty, health, sports, fishing, cars, pets, etc.

- **The Internet** — every type of media discussed above can be found on the Internet. It is usually the first place people go to look for information.

Advertisements — media messages that are designed to get your attention to get you to buy something. You can find advertisements in newspapers, on television, on the Internet, in magazines and on billboards.

Facts and Opinions in Advertisements — we learned how to identify facts and opinions in advertisements in this chapter.

- A **fact** is a true statement that can be proven by observation or research.

- An **opinion** is an attitude or viewpoint about something that cannot be proven true or false. Opinions sometimes include key phrases such as *I feel*, *I think* and *in my opinion*. They can also use words like *best*, *worst*, *favorite*, *number one*, etc.

Persuasion — an attempt to form or change a person's opinion about something. We covered five different kinds of persuasion used in advertisements in this chapter:

- **Generalization** — when advertisements generalize, they state that what is true for *one* person, is true for *all* people.

- **Bandwagon** — an appeal to follow the crowd. Advertisers use bandwagon to try to make viewers or readers feel if they don't join in, they will be left out or behind.

- **Scare Tactics** — advertisements that try to scare you into buying a product.

- **Testimonials** — advertisements that use famous people to sell a product.

- **Exaggeration** — advertisements that make products seem bigger and better than they actually are to make them more appealing.

Fine print — small writing usually found on the back or at the bottom of a product. The fine print gives you the details of an offer or the nutritional information on food products.

CHAPTER 6 REVIEW

Answer the following questions.

1. **Carla is looking for activities to do in her area over the weekend. Where would be the BEST place to look?**

    A. a magazine

    B. the television

    C. a newspaper

    D. the phone book

Sister Driving You Crazy!!? Get The SISTER-BE-GONE-ALARM!!!! New and Improved!! *With The Push of a Button Sends Out An Annoying Sound Only Sisters Can Hear!! Get The SISTER-BE-GONE-ALARM And Your Troubles Are Gone!!!

*Product does not actually keep sisters away. Instructions included. Package includes one plastic horn that lights up. Does not make any sound. No refunds.

2. **What does the SISTER-BE-GONE-ALARM promise to do?**

    A. annoy everyone in the neighborhood

    B. help you with homework

    C. protect your bike

    D. annoy sisters and keep them away

3. **What will you find in the box?**

    A. a neat alarm that will keep sisters away

    B. a plastic horn that lights up

    C. a garage door opener

    D. a cell phone

4. **The purpose of this advertisement is to**

    A.   persuade readers to buy the product.

    B.   teach readers the value of patience.

    C.   educate readers about alarms.

    D.   persuade readers to spend more time with sisters.

5. **According to the fine print, the product**

    A.   is guaranteed to work.

    B.   comes with headphones.

    C.   does not really keep sisters away.

    D.   is a great deal.

6. **A television show about how to survive in the desert comes on at 8:30 this weekend. The main purpose of this show is to**

    A.   entertain.

    B.   persuade viewers to go to the desert.

    C.   inform and entertain.

    D.   persuade viewers to stay away from the desert.

Join the Crowd and Come on Down to GameTown!! Millions have already visited our enormous store!! We have the Best Games in the World!! They are going FAST!! So get here before they're gone! Located on the corner of Peachtree and Peachtree in Atlanta. Call us toll free at 1-800-Get-Game. Open since 1995.

7. **What type of persuasion is used in this advertisement?**

   A. bandwagon

   B. testimonial

   C. generalization

   D. scare tactics

8. **Which of the following is an opinion?**

   A. Open since 1995.

   B. Located on the corner of Peachtree and Peachtree in Atlanta.

   C. Call us toll free at 1-800-Get-Game

   D. We have the Best Games in the World!!

9. **Armando is going camping with his family. Where would be the BEST place to look to for the things he will need to take on the trip?**

   A. the sports section in a newspaper

   B. a fishing magazine

   C. a camping magazine

   D. a Web site about bugs

How does she look so gorgeous? How does her skin glow? Melanie Bates, star of the hit show *Lawson's Lake,* uses DayGlo soap. "It's the only soap I trust. Try DayGlo soap, and you'll shine too."

10. **What type of persuasion is used in this ad?**

    A. bandwagon

    B. testimonial

    C. scare tactics

    D. exaggeration

Georgia 5th Grade CRCT Reading
Practice Test 1

The purpose of this practice test is to measure your progress in reading comprehension and critical thinking. This practice test is based on the Georgia standards for English and Language Arts and adheres to the sample question format provided by the Georgia Department of Education.

General Directions:

1. Read all directions carefully.

2. Read each question or sample. Then choose the best answer.

3. Choose only one answer for each question. If you change an answer, be sure to erase your original answer completely.

Each question on this test conforms to the Georgia ELA standard in the box next to it.

Creepy Crawlers or Tasty Snack?

How about chocolate covered ants and a cricket sandwich for lunch, or a large gooey water bug for a midday snack? Sound gross? Although the thought of eating insects may make you sick to your stomach, certain cultures have been eating bugs for thousands of years and continue to do so today.

More than half of the people in the world eat creepy, crawly creatures every day. There are thousands of insects that are considered <u>delicacies</u> in almost every corner of the globe. In Thailand, street vendors sell water bugs, silkworms, large insect larvae (bug eggs — like maggots) and even scorpions. In South America, concession stands offer roasted ants and chocolate covered crickets. These "treats" are actually eaten and enjoyed by many people around the world.

Many entomologists (insect scientists) agree that eating insects is not as gross as it sounds. Insects are high in protein and, if cooked the right way, can be very tasty.   Those that have tried insects are not as sickened as they thought they would be, and they even enjoyed the taste.

You may have even eaten insects yourself without even knowing it. According to some estimates, the average person eats about a pound of insects each year unintentionally. The FDA (the Food and Drug Administration), whose job it is to make sure our food is eatable, allows a small amount of insects in the food we eat. For every three and a half ounces of chocolate, for example, there may be over 60 insect parts or pieces! Too little to be tasted, but it's still there.

Since we've all <u>inadvertently</u> eaten insects at some point, why not take the next step and try something a little more daring.

Roasted scorpion anyone?

1. What is the main idea of this passage? 5RI-G 5RI-F

   A. Insects are only eaten by poor people in Asia.

   B. Insects are disgusting.

   C. Although disgusting to some, insects are eaten and enjoyed by many people.

   D. Although a delicious treat to some, eating insects can be bad for your health

2. According to the passage, what kinds of bugs do they serve in Thailand? 5RI-F

   A. flies, spiders, and gnats

   B. slugs and snails

   C. moths, caterpillars, wasps and cockroaches

   D. silkworms, larvae, water bugs and scorpions

3. What is the author's main purpose for writing this passage? 5RI-G

   A. to entertain readers with a silly story about insects

   B. to educate readers about the dangers of eating bugs

   C. to inform readers about different kinds of bugs

   D. to persuade readers to be more open-minded about bugs and try one

4. How many insect parts could there be in three and a half ounces of chocolate? 5RI-F

   A. 100   C. 600

   B. 1000   D. 60

5. What is the first sentence of the third paragraph? 5RI-B

   A. Many entomologists agree that eating bugs is not as gross as it sounds.

   B. These "treats" are actually eaten and enjoyed by many people around the world.

   C. You may have eaten insects yourself without even knowing it.

   D. More than half of the people in the world eat creepy, crawly bugs every day.

6. Which word below has the same meaning as *delicacies*? 5R3-I

   A. breakable   C. treat

   B. bite   D. scrap

7. How many pounds of insects does the average person eat in a year without even knowing it? 5RI

   A. twenty   C. five

   B. two   D. one

8. The word *inadvertently* means

   A. incorrectly.   5R3-B

   B. mistakenly.

   C. purposefully.

   D. knowingly.

You do not need to refer to the passage to answer questions 9 – 11.

9. Which word contains a prefix that means *to come in front of*?

   5R3-E
   5R3-C

   A. unfortunate

   B. misleading

   C. precede

   D. regain

10. A word that sounds like *right* but has a different meaning is

   5R3-I

   A. write

   B. plight

   C. light

   D. blight

Volcano Legends

Giant explosions of rock and smoke <u>climbing</u> into the sky! Hot, red lava slowly slithering down the side of a mountain! <u>Ash that falls like powdery snow</u> and <u>coats</u> everything for miles around! You've probably seen pictures or drawings of the results of volcanic eruptions.

Imagine how it would feel if you saw a volcano erupt right before your eyes! Well, people who lived thousands of years ago did. They were so frightened by what they saw they created stories and legends to help them explain why volcanoes erupted.

Many of these stories were about gods. To ancient people, gods were like people, they looked human and acted human, but they had incredible power. They could change the weather and could even turn themselves into animals or plants and trees!

In Rome, people believed volcanoes erupted because of Vulcan, the god of fire. They thought the hot lava and smoke erupting from a volcano were made by Vulcan's mighty hammer as he hammered thunderbolts and weapons into shape.

In Hawaii, natives believed Pele, the beautiful but easily angered Goddess of Volcanoes, caused volcanic eruptions. Pele was angry most of the time, and her anger brought about eruptions. She was respected and feared by early natives. She could cause earthquakes by stamping her feet and could start an eruption by digging into the ground with her magic stick.

In America, Native Americans told a legend about the volcano Mount St. Helens. According to legend, the volcano was once a beautiful maiden. When two brothers fell in love with her, she could not choose between them. The two men fought over her, burning villages and forests in the process. The Great Spirit, the Native American god, was furious. He changed the brothers and the woman into three mighty mountains. Whenever the brothers fight, it is said, the volcano erupts.

Early cultures told stories and legends like these to understand how and why a volcano erupts. We know a lot more today than people in ancient times. But even today, we can't accurately predict when the next volcano will erupt. Like the ancient Romans, Hawaiians, and Native Americans, we are still trying to understand volcanoes. But today we use science rather than stories and legends.

11. When Mt. St. Helens erupted in   5LSV2
    1980, which media source would
    give the LEAST up to date information?

    A. television

    B. a science journal

    C. newspaper

    D. Internet

12. Which of the following media   5LSV2-C
    sources would be the **BEST**
    place to look to learn more about volca-
    noes?

    A. a medical journal

    B. a business newspaper

    C. a science magazine

    D. an article on gardening

13. What is the main idea or theme of   5R1-G
    this passage?

    A. Volcanoes are deadly.

    B. People today believe volcanoes are
       caused by gods.

    C. Ancient people created stories to
       explain volcanic eruptions.

    D. Volcanoes never erupt.

14. What is the author's MAIN pur-   5R1-G
    pose for writing this passage?

    A. to entertain readers with interesting
       stories about volcanoes today

    B. to inform readers about how ancient
       cultures tried to explain volcanoes.

    C. to complain about the dangers of liv-
       ing next to a volcano

    D. to persuade readers to hike up a vol-
       cano

15. The word *coats* means

    A. jackets   5R3-H

    B. fur

    C. covers

    D. fills

"ash that falls like powdery snow"

16. What type of figurative language   5R1-E
    is used in this sentence?

    A. metaphor

    B. personification

    C. refrain

    D. simile

17. What is the first sentence of the   5R1-B
    fourth paragraph?

    A. Early cultures told stories and
       legends like these to understand how
       and why a volcano erupts.

    B. In Rome, people believed volcanoes
       erupted because of Vulcan, the god
       of fire.

    C. Imagine how it would feel if you
       saw a volcano erupt right before
       your eyes!

    D. Whenever the brothers fight, it is
       said, the volcano erupts.

18. People in ancient Rome believed   5R1
    volcanoes erupted because of

    A. Pele, the Goddess of Volcanoes.

    B. Mars, the god of war.

    C. Vulcan, the god of fire.

    D. two brothers fighting.

19. According to the passage, who are   5R1-F
    like humans but have amazing
    powers?

    A. Hawaiians

    B. ancient Romans

    C. Native Americans

    D. the gods

20. How many ancient peoples does the   5R1
    author discuss in the passage?

    A. one

    B. four

    C. three

    D. seven

21. Which word is an antonym for   5R3-I
    climbing?

    A. rising

    B. ascending

    C. increasing

    D. sinking

22. If you wanted to find "volcano" in   5R1-B
    a glossary, under which LETTER
    would you look?

    A. S

    B. B

    C. V

    D. E

William Blake's "Songs of Innocence: The Echoing Green"

The sun does arise,
And make happy the skies;
The merry bells ring
To welcome the Spring;
The skylark and thrush,
The birds of the bush,
Sing louder around
To the bells' cheerful sound;
While our sports shall be seen
On the echoing green.

Old John, with white hair,
Does laugh away care,
Sitting under the oak,
Among the old folk.
They laugh at our play,
And soon they all say,
'Such, such were the joys
When we all--girls and boys -
In our youth-time were seen
On the echoing green.'

Till the little ones, weary,
No more can be merry:
The sun does descend,
And our sports have an end.
Round the laps of their mothers
Many sisters and brothers,
Like birds in their nest,
Are ready for rest,
And sport no more seen
On the darkening green.

"Sitting under the oak,
Among the old folk.
They laugh at our play,
And soon they all say,"

23. What is the rhyme scheme of these lines?   5R1-H

   A. bbaa
   B. aabb
   C. aaaa
   D. abbb

24. How many stanzas are in this poem?   5R1-H

   A. 2
   B. 5
   C. 4
   D. 3

25. Which of the following lines from the poem is a refrain?   5R1-E

   A. "On the echoing green."
   B. "The sun does arise,"
   C. "The sun does descend,"
   D. "And our sports have an end."

26. Which of the following is an example of simile?   5R1-E

   A. "Old John, with white hair,/ Does laugh away care,"
   B. "Such, such were the joys/ When we all — girls and boys—"
   C. "Many sisters and brothers,/ Like birds in their nest,"
   D. "Till the little ones, weary,/ No more can be merry:"

27. What is the "echoing green" in the poem?   5R1-G

   A. a tennis court
   B. a large field
   C. a drum
   D. a tree

28. What time of year is it?   5R1-A

   A. summer
   B. fall
   C. spring
   D. winter

29. From the author's description, we can tell the children and the "old folk" are   5R1-I

   A. sad.
   B. happy.
   C. angry.
   D. nervous.

Taken from "The Treasure Hunters" by Kim Hill

It began with a simple dare. George, as usual, had started it. He'd yelled, his meaty face flushed — his small eyes narrowed, "I bet you're such a chicken you wouldn't go inta the Manchester house alone fer ten minutes!" He had been bugging me for weeks, taunting me after school, on the bus, in the hall, and I'd had enough! It was time to take a stand. No one would call me "chicken!" anymore. I took the dare. "I ain't no chicken!" I'd said. "Shoot, I'd stay fifteen minutes in that stupid house. Ten minutes is nothin'."

So, here I am, in front of the spookiest house in our town. The fact that no other kid had gone into the Manchester house before interested everyone, and all the neighborhood kids came to watch. I couldn't back down now, too many witnesses.

The Manchester house was legend in our neighborhood. Everyone knew about it, and everyone had a spooky tale to tell, told in the schoolyard and camping trips in hushed tones. It's said that old Mister Manchester, a scientist, used to perform strange experiments there. That people would go in and never come out. Then, one day, old Mister Manchester just disappeared, never to be heard from again. Whether or not any of it was true was beside the point. In matters of legend, you only had to make sure the reciting was entertaining.

The house was at the end of our five-mile town. It had once been a beautiful mansion back in the Civil War or somethin'. But now it stood in ruins: large, dark, abandoned, decrepit, and covered in cobwebs — haunted looking.

Looking at the creepy house, I wished I hadn't let George get to me, wished I didn't have to go in. Taking a deep breath, I started walking. Behind me, I heard someone yell "dead man walking!!" I stopped before I took my first step up the stairs, thinking about leaving, turning around.

"Come on Toby! Ya scared or somethin'!" George taunted from the safety of the street, far from the house.

"Yeah, Toby, ya' *really* are chicken ain't ya" joined Scooter, George's small sidekick.

"Chicken! Chicken! Chicken!" they chanted together.

"I'm goin' already! I ain't no chicken neither!" I hollered back

I walked up the steps, each one creaking loudly. I made it to the sagging front porch and put my hand on the door knob.

"Just get it over with," I said out loud.

I could still hear George and Scooter yelling "Chicken!" from the street. As soon as I turned the knob, they stopped.

Silence descended like a suffocating blanket on a hot summer night, thick and sticky. Everyone watched, holding their breath as I opened the heavy squeaking door. Gulping, I stepped into the darkened entryway, the <u>pungent</u> smell of dust, mildew, and age hitting me in the face. I looked around.

Everything was still. Not even the dust swirled from the breeze I let in. It just lay like a heavy weight on everything. The windows were covered in black grime so thick it blocked out most of the midday sun. It was so dark I could barely make out the crumbling curving staircase to my right, or the cobweb draped chandelier above my head. I closed the door behind me. The sound of the latch clicking into place and the thud of wood against wood echoed through the mansion. I felt like I was walking into a tomb with no way out.

30. Which of the following is an example of dialogue? 5R1-F

A. "Come on Toby! Ya scared or somethin'!"

B. I walked up the steps, each one creaking loudly.

C. He had been bugging me for weeks, taunting me after school, on the bus, in the hall, and I'd had enough!

D. Whether or not any of it was true was beside the point.

31. The author describes George as 5R1-I

A. kind and considerate.

B. a loud bully.

C. funny and joyful.

D. quiet and shy.

32. What is the setting of this passage? 5R1-A

A. inside a building in a big city

B. in front of the Manchester house

C. inside a barn in the country

D. on the playground at school

33. Which of the following BEST describes how Toby feels at the end of the passage? 5R1-G

A. fearless

B. secure

C. scared

D. brave

34. Who is the narrator of this passage? 5R1

    A. George
    B. Mr. Manchester
    C. the Invisible Man
    D. Toby

35. How many minutes does Toby say 5R1
    he will stay in the Manchester
    house?

    A. 15
    B. 10
    C. 5
    D. 20

"'I'm goin' already! I ain't no chicken
neither!' I hollered back."

---

36. Based on the dialogue in this pas- 5R1-D
    sage, where does Toby MOST
    likely live?

    A. in the South
    B. in the North
    C. in London
    D. in France

37. Which of the following best 5R1-A
    describes the conflict in this pas-
    sage?

    A. man verses machine
    B. man verses nature
    C. man verses man
    D. there is no conflict

38. Why does Toby go into the 5R1-G
    Manchester house?

    A. to prove he's not a chicken
    B. to impress his friends
    C. to find out if anyone lives there
    D. to prove it is not haunted

39. What does the word *pungent* 5R3-B
    mean?

    A. strong
    B. weak
    C. delightful
    D. pretty

40. When Toby comes out of the 5R1-I
    Manchester house, George will
    most likely

    A. never call him chicken again.
    B. run for president.
    C. raise money to fix the Manchester
       house.
    D. ask Toby to forgive him.

41. What is the BEST way to describe 5R1-D
    how this passage is organized?

    A. chronological order.
    B. cause and effect.
    C. compare and contrast.
    D. logical order

Lunchtime Trouble

Characters: Dad; Zack, a ten-year-old boy; Melody, Zack's thirteen-year-old sister

Scene: [*Driving down the road in the family mini-van. Dad, Zack, and Melody are trying to decide where to get lunch.*]

Dad: (*smiling at Zack and Melody*) So, what do you guys feel like having for lunch? I thought that new deli that just opened might be good.

Zack: (*looking eager and excited*) I want to go to Biggie Burger! They have a new burger. I heard about it on the television. It has fifty percent more meat, and it's all lean and a good source of protein. Can we go there, Dad?

Melody: (*cringing and sticking out her tongue as if she's gagging*) Zack, that stuff is bad for you. Dad, I can't eat there. I'm trying to stay fit for the school dance team auditions next month. Let's go someplace where I can get a salad or a sandwich.

Zack: (*trying to convince his sister*) You can get a toy there too. One of the action figures from that new film *Danger Valley*.

Melody: (*not convinced*) Zack, a toy can't make up for the yucky stuff some fast food places put in their food; stuff like sugar, artificial flavoring, fat and chemicals. I can't eat that if I want to do well in the auditions. Besides, I feel tired and sluggish after I eat stuff like that. I need to be careful about the things I eat so I feel my best.

Dad: (*looking at Melody approvingly*) I'm glad you're thinking more about good nutrition, Melody. You seem to know a lot about it. Where did you learn all this?

Melody: Oh, our dance teacher, Mrs. Fritz, talked to us about nutrition one day, and I got really interested. I started looking at the list of ingredients on the labels and read some articles in health magazines and looked on the Web for information about nutrition.

Zack: (*looking a little surprised*) Yeah, but you used to love junk food. Aren't you going to eat it anymore?

Melody: I'll eat it sometimes. A little bit isn't bad. I like snacks as much as the next person. I figure if I eat healthy most of the time I can eat treats occasionally.

Dad: That sounds like a good plan to follow. I'm sure you'll be ready for the auditions, and you'll do great. But we still need to figure out where we're going to eat.

Zack: (*pointing out the window*) Dad, that deli you were talking about is just up ahead. I'm sure they have salads, and I can get a turkey sandwich.

Dad: (*surprised*) What? You don't want to go to Biggie Burger anymore?

Zack: (*shrugging his shoulders and smiling*) A sandwich just sounds better to me now. Besides, I want to be ready for our biking trip next week. Maybe I'll even beat Melody in a race.

Melody: (*laughing*) Fat chance!

---

42. Melody used three sources to learn about nutrition. Which one of the following was NOT used?   5LSV2-C

    A. television

    B. magazines

    C. the Web

    D. reading the labels

43. When did Melody become interested in nutrition?   5R1

    A. when she saw a commercial on television

    B. after she talked to her doctor

    C. after Mrs. Fritz talked about nutrition

    D. She's never been interested in nutrition.

44. What kind of food are Melody and Zack most likely to eat from now on?   5R1-G

    A. ice cream

    B. cheeseburgers from Biggie Burger

    C. candy

    D. deli sandwiches

45. How does Melody respond to Zack's suggestion to go to Biggie Burger?   5R1-I

    A. nervously

    B. happily

    C. disgustedly

    D. angrily

46. This passage can best be described as   5R1

    A. a folk tale.

    B. nonfiction.

    C. a poem.

    D. an essay.

47. What is the setting of this passage?   5R1-A

    A. Biggie Burger

    B. a deli

    C. a mini-van

    D. a school

48. What are the "yucky" things Mel- 5R1-G
    ody says some fast food restau-
    rants put in their food?

    A. wheat germ, seaweed and algae

    B. sugar, artificial flavoring, fat and
        chemicals

    C. oils, artificial sweeteners, food col-
        oring,and butter

    D. flour, yeast, eggs and vanilla

49. How does Dad react when Zack 5R1-I
    changes his mind about going to
    Biggie Burger?

    A. annoyed and upset

    B. curious and doubtful

    C. surprised and pleased

    D. depressed and disappointed

50. How did Zack hear about the 5LSV2-B
    new burger at Biggie Burger?

    A. the newspaper

    B. the radio

    C. a book

    D. the television

Georgia 5th Grade CRCT Reading Practice Test 2

The purpose of this practice test is to measure your progress in reading comprehension and critical thinking. This practice test is based on the Georgia standards for English and Language Arts and adheres to the sample question format provided by the Georgia Department of Education.

General Directions:

1. Read all directions carefully.

2. Read each question or sample. Then choose the best answer.

3. Choose only one answer for each question. If you change an answer, be sure to erase your original answer completely.

Each question on this test conforms to the Georgia ELA standard in the box next to it.

Life on Mars

Was there ever life on Mars? New discoveries suggest there may have been. Evidence suggests that Mars did have water on it at one time, and that it could have <u>supported</u> some sort of life. Scientists have found many clues that suggest this is true. One of the most important was the discovery of an ancient shoreline of a large Martian sea. The area where the sea would have been is level and flat where mud and silt may have built up. There are also gullies (deep ruts or ditches) on the surface of the planet that were most likely caused by water. Scientists think that rushing water may have carved or worn away the soil, creating large crater walls. Scientists have also discovered that Martian rocks have a different makeup because of the presence of water.

1. What is the main idea of this paragraph? 5R1-G

   A. There is evidence that water and possibly life existed on Mars.

   B. Mars is called the red planet.

   C. There is a lot of water on Mars today.

   D. There is no proof that water was ever on Mars.

2. What are the supporting details in this passage? 5R1-F

   A. Mars had water on it at some time.

   B. Mars could have supported some form of life.

   C. ancient shoreline, level where sea was, gullies, crater walls, different makeup of Martian rocks

   D. scientists, Martians, and radio waves

3. What does the word *supported* mean in this passage? 5R3-B

   A. provided for

   B. leaned against

   C. fought with

   D. left alone

4. Why do scientists believe Mars may have had life on it? 5R1 5LSV2

   A. because they found Martian fossils

   B. because they found rocks with footprints

   C. because they found eggs

   D. because they found out it once had water

5. What was one of the most important clues scientists found?

5R1-F
5R1

   A.   Martian rock

   B.   the ancient shoreline of a sea

   C.   gullies made by water

   D.   large craters made by water

6. Which of the following would be
the BEST place to look if you
wanted to learn more about water and life
on Mars?

5LSV2-C

   A.   a race car magazine

   B.   a dictionary

   C.   a science fiction book

   D.   a science article

You do not need to refer to the passage to answer questions 7 and 8.

7. Which word contains a suffix that
means an amount or quantity that
fills something?

5R3-C
5R3-E

   A.   mouthful

   B.   capable

   C.   contentment

   D.   reporter

8. Which word contains a prefix that
means in place of or alternate?

5R3-C
5R3-E

   A.   immediate

   B.   instead

   C.   unable

   D.   distrust

Fred Begay: The Hard Walk

Fred Begay was only nine when his mother took him to the river near where they lived. "We have no food," she said, "but if you follow that river 50 miles, you will find food and a place to stay." A few days later, he arrived at the Indian Affairs School. For two years, he did not see his parents. Years later, Begay would become the first Navajo to become a doctor of physics.

Begay was born on a reservation in the West. Begay's father and mother were Native American. They were from the Navajo tribe. They did not own a house, but traveled from place to place, sleeping in a tent or out in the open. Begay learned how to hunt, and his parents taught him how to tell time by looking at the sun. Begay and his family all spoke Navajo.

When Begay entered the Indian Affairs School, he felt as if he had entered a different world. It was his first meeting with white people. All the students had to wear uniforms. He could not speak his language, Navajo, but was taught English instead. He was not allowed to practice the ceremonies his parents had taught him. Begay even had to change his name!

The school taught students a trade. Begay learned farming and English. But Begay spoke English poorly. He could only read on a second grade level. He wanted to learn more, but the Indian Affairs School offered very little.

Begay's big break came when he received a letter saying that there were scholarships available to Navajos who wanted to go to college. Begay jumped at the chance. In 1955, he entered the University of New Mexico. At first, the university did not want to accept him. The only way he could <u>attend</u> was to go to college during the day and finish high school at night. Begay was excited to be there, even though he had to work very hard to catch up with the other students. He discovered he liked science and pursued a degree in it. He received his first degree in 1961 and his second in 1963.

Begay worked for NASA, the National Aeronautics and Space Administration, during the 1960s. In 1971, he became a doctor of physics. He was the first Navajo to ever do so.

Since then, Begay has strived to improve education for children living on reservations. He has improved the math and science programs at all Navajo high schools. He has also helped direct a million dollar math and science project at Arizona State University.

Begay has won many awards for the work he has done to help Navajo children excel in math and science. In 1994, he won the National Science Foundations Lifetime Achievement Award.

9. What is the implied main idea of   5R1-F
   this passage?

   A. Fred Begay worked hard to get his
      education and to improve education
      for Navajo children.

   B. Fred Begay went to school to get
      away from his parents and the reser-
      vation.

   C. Fred Begay thought learning was
      only for rich people.

   D. Fred Begay walked 50 miles to find
      food and shelter.

10. What happened FIRST?   5R1-F
                            5R1

   A. Fred Begay attended the
      Indian Affairs School.

   B. Fred Begay received his first degree.

   C. Fred Begay went to the University
      of New Mexico.

   D. Fred Begay walked 50 miles.

11. How has Fred Begay's work helped   5R1-F
    Navajo children today?   5R1-G

   A. Math and science programs have
      improved on all Navajo
      reservations.

   B. Children no longer have to do
      household chores.

   C. Children can choose how long lunch
      and recess will be.

   D. Math and science are not taught on
      Navajo reservations.

12. What did Begay learn at the Indian   5R1
    Affairs School?

   A. dancing and singing

   B. football and hockey

   C. farming and English

   D. sewing and needlepoint

13. Why did Begay go to the Indian   5R1-F
    Affairs School?

   A. because his family had no food

   B. because he wanted to learn about
      farming

   C. because he was staying with his aunt

   D. because his father worked there

14. The word *attend* means   5R3-H

   A. go to.

   B. listen.

   C. miss.

   D. absent.

15. What is the topic sentence of the   5R1-B
    second paragraph?

   A. Begay, his four brothers, and his
      parents all spoke Navajo.

   B. Since then, Begay has strived to
      improve education for children liv-
      ing on reservations.

   C. Begay was born on a reservation in
      the West.

   D. When Begay entered the Indian
      Affairs School, he felt as if he had
      entered a different world.

16. What Native American tribe were   5R1
    Begay's parents from?

   A. Cherokee

   B. Chippewa

   C. Creek

   D. Navajo

17. What is the author's MAIN reason   5R1-G
for writing "Fred Begay: The Hard
Walk"?

   A. to persuade readers to visit
reservations

   B. to inform readers about Fred
Begay's life

   C. to entertain readers with a funny
story

   D. to convince readers walking 50
miles is hard.

18. This passage can best be described   5R1
as

   A. a poem.

   B. a fable.

   C. fiction.

   D. nonfiction.

19. Which of the following BEST   5R1-D
describes how this passage is organized?

   A. cause and effect

   B. compare and contrast

   C. chronological

   D. there is no order

20. How did Fred Begay MOST likely   5R1-I
feel when he first entered the
Indian Affairs School?

   A. mad and rebellious

   B. unsure and alien

   C. happy and grateful

   D. confident and protected

Sack Lunches

The large clock in the center of town struck twelve. Ding! Dong! Ding! Dong! It was everyone's cue to have lunch. "I've got a wonderful lunch packed for us today," says my great aunt Georgia. I call her Aunt G. "Sandwiches and apples and something sweet," she smiles down at me. I love having lunch with Aunt G. She always makes the best things, packed neatly into brown paper bags. Today, we're going to the park to eat lunch.

As we walk, we pass the old fabric mill. It was turned into an apartment building when the mill closed down years ago. Auntie says, "I remember going in there when it was a mill. I was a child. We were poor back then. But most people were at that time because of the Great Depression. My sister, your grandma, would always go to the mill to take lunch to Daddy right before that clock would strike twelve.

"One day I went with her. I carried Daddy's lunch sack and walked behind her.

"When we went in, I saw a huge room. There were machines everywhere. The noise was very loud. I could hear steam hissing, metal parts grinding and pumps pumping. It was such a chorus of noise!

"People sat close together on long benches, or stood side by side as they worked. There were even children who worked there.

"Your grandma, who was used to the sights and sounds of the mill, ran ahead of me looking for Daddy. I tried to yell to her, but it was so noisy I could barely hear my own voice. So I started running after her, being careful not to bump any-one or trip on anything. I kept my eyes on the ground to make sure I didn't and wound up bumping right into Daddy!

"He swept me up in his arms and asked, 'what are you doing here? Come to help?'

I replied 'I brought you lunch Daddy.'

"He looked in the sack, 'why, you did. You brought sandwiches and an apple. That's my good girl,' he said, hugging me."

"I took Daddy's lunch to him every day from then on," Aunt G says.

"Speaking of lunch, my girl, you must be hungry. Let's sit here and eat." We are at the park already, standing next to a large cherry tree, heavy with pink blossoms. "This looks like a good spot," she says, spreading a checkered blanket on the ground. I look at the brown sack she had been carrying while we walked, and my stomach growled.

"It's perfect, Aunt G," I reply.

21. What is the theme of "Sack Lunches"? 5R1-G

    A. What people eat for lunch has changed a lot over the years.

    B. Making lunch for and eating lunch with a loved one can make you feel safe and happy, no matter where you are.

    C. Mills are dangerous places to eat lunch.

    D. People who worked at mills were grateful they had a lunch to eat.

22. What is the setting of Aunt G's story about taking lunch to her Daddy? 5R1-A

    A. in her mother's house

    B. on a farm

    C. in the mill

    D. in the mall

23. Why were most people poor when Aunt G was a little girl? 5R1-D

    A. because of the Great Depression

    B. because no one wanted to work

    C. because they didn't care about money

    D. because they ran out of paper

24. What will the girl and Aunt G MOST likely do next? 5R1-G

    A. They will eat lunch.

    B. They will shop for clothes.

    C. They will take a nap.

    D. They will fight over a sandwich.

"I could hear steam hissing"

25. What type of figurative language is used in this phrase? 5R1-E

    A. refrain

    B. simile

    C. hyperbole

    D. personification

26. The author describes Aunt G as 5R1-F

    A. warm and kind.

    B. shy and scared.

    C. loud and mean.

    D. serious and quiet.

27. What did Aunt G pack for lunch at the park?   5R1

   A.   cheese and crackers

   B.   fried chicken, corn, and banana pudding

   C.   sandwiches, apples, and something sweet

   D.   lasagna and garlic bread

28. Why did Aunt G go into the mill?   5R1-F

   A.   to find her sister

   B.   to work

   C.   to get fabric

   D.   to take lunch to her daddy

29. Where do Aunt G and her niece have lunch?   5R1-A

   A.   in the kitchen

   B.   at a restaurant

   C.   in the mill

   D.   at the park

30. When Aunt G first goes into the mill, she is   5R1-I

   A.   confused and a little scared by the machines and the noise.

   B.   terrified and unable to move because of all the people.

   C.   talkative and hyper.

   D.   lonesome and homesick.

31. Which of the following is an example of dialogue?   5R1-F

   A.   I love having lunch with Aunt G.

   B.   We were at the park already, standing next to a large cherry tree, heavy with pink blossoms.

   C.   "I took Daddy's lunch to him everyday from then on," Aunt G says.

   D.   Today, we're going to the park to eat lunch.

32. What is the second sentence of the second paragraph?   5R1-B

   A.   Ding! Dong! Ding! Dong!

   B.   It was turned into an apartment building when the mill closed down years ago.

   C.   We were poor back then.

   D.   As we walk, we pass the old fabric mill.

A Little Boy's Dream
by Katherine Mansfield

To and fro, to and fro
In my little boat I go
Sailing far across the sea
All alone, just little me.
And the sea is big and strong
And the journey very long.
To and fro, to and fro
In my little boat I go.

Sea and sky, sea and sky,
Quietly on the deck I lie,
Having just a little rest.
I have really done my best
In an awful pirate fight,
But we captured them all right.
Sea and sky, sea and sky,
Quietly on the deck I lie —

Far away, far away
From my home and from my play,
On a journey without end
Only with the sea for friend
And the fishes in the sea.
But they swim away from me
Far away, far away
From my home and from my play.

Then he cried "O, Mother dear."
And he woke and sat upright,
They were in the rocking chair,
Mother's arms around him — tight.

33. How many stanzas are there in this poem?   5R1-H

    A. 4   C. 2
    B. 3   D. none

34. Which of the following is one of the refrains in the passage?   5R1-E

    A. "Only with the sea for friend
         And the fishes in the sea."

    B. "And the sea is big and strong
         And the journey very long."

    C. "I have really done my best
         In an awful pirate fight,"

    D. "To and fro, to and fro
         In my little boat I go."

35. Each line of the passage starts with   5R1-H

    A. a lower case letter.
    B. a period.
    C. a capital letter.
    D. quotation marks.

> "Sea and sky, sea and sky"

36. What type of sound effect is used in this line?   5R1-H

    A. alliteration
    B. onomatopoeia
    C. metaphor
    D. simile

37. Why did the little boy cry "O, Mother dear"? 5R1-I

    A. because he was frightened

    B. because he wanted to get a bigger boat

    C. because he needed help with homework

    D. because he was asleep

38. Which word is an antonym of *journey*? 5R3-I

    A. trip

    B. excursion

    C. voyage

    D. confinement

39. Which of the following BEST describes how the boy feels at the end of the passage? 5R1-G

    A. secure and safe

    B. alone and afraid

    C. brave and strong

    D. old and wise

40. Where does the little boy have his dream? 5R1-A

    A. in a little boat

    B. in a rocking chair

    C. in his bed

    D. in a treehouse

You do not need to refer to the passage to answer question 41.

41. The tension or crisis in a plot is called 5R1-A

    A. the conflict.

    B. the setting.

    C. the resolution.

    D. characterization.

Tricks of the Trade

How many advertisements do you think you see a day? Twenty? Thirty? You see many more than that, most likely. If you're the average kid, you spend over four hours a day watching television, surfing the Internet, flipping through magazines or listening to the radio. These are all forms of media, and they all contain advertisements. The messages advertisements send affect what you decide to buy or ask your parents to buy, from clothing and food to toys and video games.

The people who create advertisements spend a lot of time thinking about what looks "cool" to you. They try to make commercials entertaining to get your attention. They make their product the "star" of the advertisement. They dress it up, put it under bright lights and make it look as good as they can. Their sole purpose is to persuade you to buy whatever they're selling — whether it's good for you or not.

Famous people like Tiger Woods are in commercials to convince viewers they will be better at sports if they wear the same brand of hat or shoes he wears. Cartoon characters show up in sugary cereal ads telling viewers it's "part of a balanced diet and a good source of calcium." Pictures of fast food restaurants are in popular PlayStation and X-Box video games to get players to eat there. All of these are examples of how advertisements can be misleading. The reality is practice makes you better at sports — not wearing what Tiger Woods wears. And the truth is adding calcium to a sugary cereal does not make it good for you.

Advertisements can be tricky. Sometimes it can be hard to decide which ones are honest and which ones are misleading. Do a little detective work. The next time you see an advertisement, look at it closely and ask yourself the following questions:

- Who created this message?
- How did it get my attention, what techniques did they use?
- How would different people look at this message?
- What values and points of view are in this message? What's left out and why?
- Why is this message being sent?

Don't be fooled by tricky advertisements. Look closely at the advertisements you see. Once you do, you may not want to "buy it" anymore.

42. Based on the passage, advertisers   5R1
    spend a lot of time thinking about

    A. what looks "cool" and attractive to
        viewers.

    B. how to make more money.

    C. what will help children do better in
        school.

    D. how to get children to eat less sugar.

43. How do advertisements get   5LSV2-B
    viewers' attention?

    A. They hypnotize them.

    B. They entertain them.

    C. They put them to sleep.

    D. They tell jokes.

44. Which of the following is one of   5LSV2-C
    the questions you should ask
    when you see an advertisement?

    A. How long will this last?

    B. How soon can I get one?

    C. Why is it so expensive?

    D. Why is this message being sent?

45. How many hours a day does the   5LSV2
    average child spend watching tele-
    vision, surfing the Internet or flipping
    through magazines and listening to the
    radio?

    A. one hour

    B. six hours

    C. over four hours

    D. under three hours

46. Based on the passage, what kind of   5R1
    advertisements can you find in video
    games?

    A. ads for fast food restaurants

    B. ads for toothpaste

    C. ads for chewing gum

    D. ads for sneakers

47. What is the author's MAIN reason   5R1-G
    for writing "Tricks of the Trade?"

    A. to convince children to never buy
        anything

    B. to complain about video games

    C. to persuade children to look closely
        at what they see in advertisements

    D. to inform children of the dangers of
        watching too much television

48. In this passage, the word *sole*   5R3-H
    means

    A. the bottom of a shoe

    B. a spirit

    C. a bunch

    D. only

49. The author mentions four kinds of   5LSV2
    media in the passage. Which of
    the following was NOT used?

    A. television

    B. magazines

    C. newspapers

    D. the Internet

50. According to the passage, children   5R1-G
    should

    A. always believe what advertisements say.

    B. question what they see in advertisements.

    C. never watch advertisements on television.

    D. make their own advertisements.